Achieving
PLANNED
INNOVATION®

A PROVEN SYSTEM FOR
CREATING SUCCESSFUL NEW
PRODUCTS AND SERVICES

FRANK R. BACON, JR.
THOMAS W. BUTLER, JR.

THE FREE PRESS

New York   London   Toronto   Sydney   Singapore

PLANNED INNOVATION®

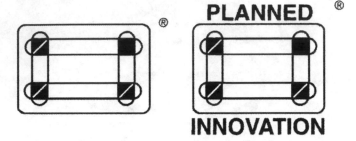

All are registered service marks of Dr. Frank R. Bacon.

THE FREE PRESS
A Division of Simon & Schuster Inc.
1230 Avenue of the Americas
New York, NY 10020

THE FREE PRESS and colophon are trademarks
of Simon & Schuster Inc.

Manufactured in the United States of America

10   9   8   7   6   5   4   3   2   1

Library of Congress Cataloging-in-Publication Data

Bacon, Frank R.
    Achieving planned innovation : a proven system for creating successful new
products and services / Frank R. Bacon, Jr., Thomas W. Butler, Jr.
        p.   cm.
    Rev. ed. of: Planned innovation. 2nd ed.   1981.
    Includes bibliographical references and index.
    ISBN 978-1-416-57321-0
    1. New products—Management.   2. Production planning.   3. Product
management.   4. Marketing research.   I. Butler, Thomas W.   II. Bacon,
Frank R.   Planned innovation.   III. Title.
    HF5415. 153.B33   1988
    658.5'75—dc21   97-25141
                                                              CIP

Contents

Prologue: How Planned Innovation
Was Developed and Where It Has Been Used   xi

1. What This Book Is All About   1

    Example 1: What We Mean By a High Rate of Success   2
    Example 2: Achieving Accelerated, Sustained Growth   3
    Example 3: Growth Through Improvements in Existing Products 5
    Example 4: Providing Guidance to R&D   6
    Would Planned Innovation Have Value to Your Firm?   7

2. What Is Planned Innovation?   9

3. The Planned Innovation System   13

    Element One: A Disciplined Scientific Reasoning Process   13
    Element Two: Lasting Marketing Orientation   15
    Element Three: Proper Selection Criteria   16
    Element Four: Using Scientific Reasoning to Determine
        Requirements Before Making Major Expenditures   17
    Element Five: Ensure Multifunctional Involvement   18

4. Establishing a Disciplined Scientific
    Reasoning Process for New Product Innovation   19

5. The Model of Requirements for
    Successful Innovation   26

    Model for Identifying Economic and Emotive Value   31
    Four Questions to Address in Each Segment of Focus   35
    Opportunity Selection Criteria Become the Optimizing Function   36

6. Forming a Lasting Market Orientation   39

    Definition of Business Orientations   39
    Blue Jeans—a Universal Example   41
    Functional Product-Market Definition   44
    Definition of "Product"   45
    Definition of "Functional Need"   45
    Definition of "Customer"   46
    Definition of "Geography"   47
    Marketing Strategy, Mix, and Plan   47
    Examples of Functional Product-Market
        Definitions for Blue Jeans   49
    Changing to a Market Orientation   51

7. The Value of Opportunity Selection Criteria   53

    Selection versus Screening Criteria   55
    Selection Criteria Can Also Be Used for Screening   57
    Issues Involved in Opportunity Selection Process   57
    Importance of Integrating Strategy and Tactics   59
    Matching Resources to Opportunities   60
    Success Must Be Tactical and Strategic   60

8. Obtaining Proper Inputs to
    Opportunity Selection Criteria   64

    Mission Statements Guide New Product Innovation   65
    Statement of Financial Goals Needed   66

The Role of Functional Objectives 67
Defining Capabilities, Strengths, and Weaknesses 67
Competitive Opening and Advantage 73
External Trends 76
The Mental Work Required Is Well Worth the Effort 79

9. The Power of Scientific Thought Process in
   New Product Opportunity Analysis 80

The Technique of Strong Inference 82
The Benefit of Hypotheses of Cause-Effect 85
Scientifically Based Opportunity Analysis Can Be Valuable at
   Any Stage of New Product Development 88

10. Opportunity Analysis: Initial Assessment Phase 91

First, Define the Opportunity 93
Second, Verify that Opportunity Meets Selection Criteria
   and Establish Priority 96
Third, Identify Critical Issues 98
Fourth, Formulate Hypotheses Based on Critical Issues 98
Fifth, Determine What Information Would Provide the
   Most Decisive Test of Hypotheses 99
Sixth, Go for the Jugular in Obtaining Information 100
What Should Be Accomplished in the Initial Assessment Phase 102

11. Opportunity Analysis: Range of Requirements Phase 104

Testing Hypotheses Regarding Range of Requirements 107
Sample Size Required 108
Need for a Carefully Structured Questionnaire 109
Analysis of Competition 110
What Should Be Accomplished in the
   Range of Requirements Phase 113

12. Opportunity Analysis: Quantitative Confirmation
    of Market Potential Phase 116

Design of a Stratified Random Sample 120

What Should Be Accomplished in the
   Quantitative Confirmation Phase   123

13. Application of Opportunity Analysis to
    Different Types of Products and Markets   124

    Parallel Activities Are Possible   128
    Determining Requirements for Consumer Products   128

14. Implementing Planned Innovation to Achieve
    Multifunctional Involvement   134

    Managerial Support Required 135
    Multifunctional Involvement   135
    Qualification and Training of Analysts   136
    Maintaining the Flow of Ideas   138
    Implementing the Planned Innovation System   141
    The Planned Innovation Board   143
    Recurrent Training   144

    Epilogue: How Planned Innovation Provides
    Answers to Popular Myths Regarding
    New Product Innovation   147

    Nine Areas of Requirements for Successful Innovation   147
    Myth 1: The Better Mousetrap   148
    Myth 2: Another Xerox   149
    Myth 3: The Gift of Genius   151
    Myth 4: The Lotto   151
    Myth 5: All You Have to Do Is Ask Your Customer   152
    Myth 6: The Alchemist Stone   154

    Notes   155

Prologue

How Planned Innovation Was Developed and Where It Has Been Used

During the past four decades, we, the authors, have maintained an active professional interest in new product innovation. We have now achieved an insight into the process from almost every perspective. Both of us have held full-time positions in industry, yet have also supervised university research on the subject, taught graduate-level courses on the subject, and given many seminars on strategic planning and new product development. In addition, we have combined our different talents to work as problem-solvers and teacher-consultants to scores of firms interested in improving the speed, efficiency, and success of new product innovation.

We pioneered the development and teaching of a graduate-level course in new product innovation for a combined class of engineering and business students at Michigan State University, which we continued to teach for a decade.[1] Since then, most of our efforts have been in off-campus executive education and in coaching management teams using Planned Innovation.

We first worked together as electronic engineers on a government-sponsored research program at the University of Michigan, developing electronic countermeasures equipment and systems for the U.S. Army. Our exposure to information theory applied to the detection of signals in noise, and to the problems of identifying unmet needs beyond the understanding of our customers (Army commanders), contributed largely to the conceptual basis for Planned Innovation.

With similar undergraduate training (electronic engineers), but with different advanced training, we have always functioned well as a team. Dr. Bacon holds a Bachelor of Science degree in Electrical Engineering from Purdue University and a Master's degree and Ph.D. from the University of Michigan, where he specialized in marketing and quantitative research methods. He was the founder of the Industrial Development Division of the Institute of Science and Technology and served as its first Research Program Director. The work he initiated there toward the development of an improved theoretical framework for new product development decisions provided the foundation for the Needs-Requirements model which is at the heart of the Planned Innovation process. He is a founding member of the Product Development and Management Association, and he has been a professor of Marketing in the Graduate School of Business at Michigan State University since 1965 (on adjunct status since 1981).

Dr. Butler's training is exclusively technical in nature. He received all degrees—Bachelor of Science in Electrical Engineering, Master's degree in Physics, and Ph.D. in Electrical Engineering—from the University of Michigan. Formerly a professor of Electrical Engineering at the University of Michigan and director of the Cooley Laboratory, a major electronics research laboratory in the university serving both industry and government, Dr. Butler served as corporate Vice President of Engineering and Research and Chief Technical Officer at AMF, Inc. He has also held the position of vice presiden/technical director of the Genlyte Group and later served as dean of Engineering and Computer Science at Oakland University.

Led by our technical backgrounds, we initially used the Planned Innovation procedures in industries and product fields involving high technology including electronic computer mainframe and peripheral devices, scientific instruments, optical coatings, electronic and electromechanical components, materials-handling equipment, industrial controls for machine tools, automotive components, building supplies and equipment, and snow-making equipment. Following the publication of the first edition of *Planned Innovation* in 1973, we expanded our work to include in our second edition a number of consumer products manufactured by AMF in the recreation equipment field, such as bicycles, skis, golf clubs, and boats and marine accessories.

Most of our time during the past two decades has been spent with large, multidivisional, multinational firms, which may consist of fifty or more separate businesses, each having its own business team requiring separate attention. Even though we have not worked with *every* team in such companies, we have assisted with the application of at least some aspects of Planned Innovation in hundreds of diverse businesses representing many more products than that.

As was the case with the first and second editions, this third book is not a research study. Rather, it is a statement of our philosophy of approach, together with well-tested procedures, for successful product innovation. We now do have the results of an independent study of the outstanding effectiveness of our procedures at the Dow Chemical Company, which we present in Chapter 1.

A summary of the major firms and their products with which we have had different degrees of involvement is shown below, categorized by size (large, medium, and small firms). Firms with which we have had high levels of involvement are shown with an asterisk.

LARGE COMPANIES

ALFA Industries (Mexico)

- *Retail distribution*

AMF*

- *Bicycles*
- *Golf clubs*
- *Boats*
- *Golf carts*
- *Motorcycles*
- *Gymnastics equipment*

Allied Signal

- *Aerospace communication and navigation equipment*
- *Aircraft components*

Bell & Howell

- *Automatic materials handling systems*

Cordemex (Mexico)

- *Sisal products*

Dow Corning*

- *Silicone products*
- *Caulking*
- *Sealing*
- *Roofing*
- *Hoses*

Dow Chemical*

- *Chemicals*
- *Plastics*
- *Engineering thermoplastics*

IBM

- *Small business computers*
- *Other computers*

Lear Siegler, Inc. (now Smith Industries)*

- *Mailmobile*
- *Data transfer module*
- *Aircraft navigation and guidance*
- *Aviation fuel pumps*
- *Land vehicle navigation*
- *Aviation power generation*

Owens Corning Fiberglass

- *Bath showers*
- *Tubs*
- *Other fiberglass products*

Owens Illinois*

- *Solar energy products*
- *Food packaging*

Schlumberger

- *Electro-optical gauging*

Steelcase

- *Office furniture systems*

Toledo Scale*

- *Electronic retail grocery scales*
- *Electronic digital parts counters*
- *Automatic prepack scales*

MEDIUM COMPANIES

Asbjorn Habberstad (Norway)

- *Ergonomic computer terminals*

Donnelly Mirrors*

- *Auto mirror systems*
- *Optical coatings*
- *Moon roofs and molded windows for autos*

Federal Screw Works*

- *Electronic speech synthesis*
- *Handi Voice*
- *Computer Aided Instruction*

MACtac (subsidiary of Bemis)*

- *Pressure-sensitive films*
- *Labels*
- *Adhesives*

Mechanical Products

- *Circuit breakers for aircraft, trucks, and industrial equipment*

Rospatch

- *Labels and tapes*
- *Label equipment*
- *Packaging*

Simmonds Precision

- *Aircraft gauging systems*
- *Aircraft engine wiring harnesses*

SMALL COMPANIES

GRID Publishing, Inc.

- *Textbooks and professional journals*

Irwin Seating

- *Auditorium seating*
- *Theater seating*
- *Stadium seating*

Leco

- *Infrared gas analyzers*
- *Oxygen analyzers*
- *Nitrogen analyzers*
- *Gas chromatography*

Motor Products Owosso*

- *Electric trolling motors*
- *Industrial DC motors*
- *Lawnmower and snowblower starting motors*
- *"Kangaroo Caddy" golf cart*

Oliver Products

- *Specialty adhesives*
- *Special equipment*
- *Bread slicers*

Sarns, Inc.

- *Intravenous pumps*
- *Heart stress testing*
- *Disposable medical products*
- *Life support equipment for open heart surgery*

XYCOM

- *Industrial computer terminals*

Dr. Frank R. Bacon, Jr.
Dr. Thomas W. Butler, Jr.

Acknowledgements

Many businessmen and women, graduate students, colleagues, and associates have contributed to the development and refinement of Planned Innovation over the years. For specific help in the preparation of this third edition, the authors wish to acknowledge and express appreciation to their long-time friends and associates, Joseph E. Szalay and R. Trezevant Wigfall, who read the manuscript and have made many helpful suggestions over the years.

We are also indebted to the many individuals and firms that contributed case materials and illustrations used throughout the text. These include: Dr. Clive P. Bosnyak, senior associate scientist, The Dow Chemical Company; Barry L. Casey, manager, Marketing/New Business Development and Planning, Smith Industries (formerly Lear Siegler Inc.); Richard E. Cook, president, Cascade Engineering; Donivan Hall, former director, Research, Development and Engineering, Toledo Scale (now Mettler-Toledo, Inc.); Elmar Klotz, former president, Avionics Group, AlliedSignal Aerospace; James A. Knister, senior vice president, Donnelly Corporation; William W. Sorenson, chairman, American Sports Products Group Inc., former president, American Athletics Division, AMF (now American Athletics, Inc.); Greg Stevens, president, WinOvations, Inc.; and Peter R. Styles, vice president, European Government Affairs, ENRON Capital and Trade Resources. We also express appreciation to Dr. E. Jerome McCarthy for contributions regarding product-market definition and market-oriented strategy planning. We are also indebted to Dr. William K. Meade, assistant professor of Marketing, University of Missouri—St. Louis, who called attention to the similarity between our methodologies and the technique of strong inference used by early scientists, and the similarity between Planned Innovation and entrepreneurship as defined by economist Israel Kirzner.

In addition, we also thank others who read the preliminary manuscript and made helpful suggestions. These include: sons Christopher W. Bacon, application specific integrated circuits engineer, Hewlett-Packard Company, and Dr. Donald R. Bacon, associate professor of Marketing at the University of Denver; Anthony J. Carbone, group vice president, Dow Plastics, The Dow Chemical Company; D. Thomas Eastham, formerly professor of mathematics, Western Oregon State College; Lynne M. Galligan, technical director, General Electric Corporate Research and Development; Bob Mlnarik, vice chairman, Bemis Company, Inc., president and CEO Mactac (Morgan Adhesives Company); Michael D. Parker, group vice president, Chemicals and Performance Products and Hydrocarbons and Energy, The Dow Chemical Company; John E. Plott, corporate new business market development manager, Dow Corning Corporation; Dr. Robert W. Nason, professor of marketing and chairperson, marketing and supply chain management, Eli Broad Graduate School of Management, Michigan State University; Donald N. Smith, associate director, Manufacturing Systems, Office for the Study of Automotive Transportation, University of Michigan Transportation Research Institute; Dr. Otto Soskuty, formerly chief of engineering industries, United Nations Industrial Development Organization, Vienna; Kim A. Stewart, assistant professor of management, University of Denver; and Robert Thele, president, Sport Court, Inc. a subsidiary of American Sports Products Group Inc.

Additional thanks go to our editor, Jo-Ann Pepperl, for making many improvements and suggestions, to our typists Patricia Rapley and Rebecca Hulburt, and to our wives, Kathleen and Jeanne, who offered encouragement and support throughout the writing process.

1

What This Book Is All About

The message of this book is simple: High rates of success in new product innovation are possible for any firm, of any size, in any country in the world. Planned innovation is a proven, action-oriented, results-producing recipe for achieving such success. The purpose of this book is to explain the philosophy and procedures which lead to that success.

Do any of the following four scenarios fit your firm's situation?

1. Your firm already has a new product development process which is not functioning smoothly and efficiently, and/or is not producing a high rate of success.

2. Your firm has recently decided it needs accelerated sustained growth through new product developments (possibly because the benefits from a reengineering or cost reduction program have been exhausted, leaving a need for increased profit from accelerated growth).

3. Your firm has concluded that, despite its suitable position in existing product-markets, it needs to modify and extend its current products to maintain or expand its future position in these markets.

4. Your firm has a central or regional R & D group which is operating with little or no input regarding future product-markets.

If you answered yes to any of the four questions, you should read on. The examples given will illustrate how Planned Innovations addresses each of these situations.

Example #1: What We Mean by a High Rate of Success

A ninety-seven percent (97%) commercial success rate is the conclusion from a recent study of the effectiveness of Planned Innovation at The Dow Chemical Company. Amazing, astounding, unbelievable results? Here is a summary of the study's conclusions, in the words of Greg Stevens, former opportunity analyst at Dow, and now president of WinOvations, Inc., of Midland, Michigan.

> As part of my independent work, I had occasion to carefully quantify the returns to The Dow Chemical Company over a ten-year period from implementing the Planned Innovation procedures which you have developed. This is the only time such a quantification has been done. It required a great deal of effort, because so many projects were done (277) by so many individuals (73) over such a long time period, both in North America and Europe. Ultimately, I was able to quantify virtually the entire sample.
>
> Key findings from this analysis follow:
>
> 1. Ninety-seven percent (97%) of the positive recommendations which the businesses developed made money (33 of 34 projects developed). These results show that it is possible to determine with near certainty which opportunities to develop, even when commercializing substantially new products.
>
> 2. The cumulative profits earned (as measured by return on sales) using the Planned Innovation process have exceeded $200 million over a ten-year period, and are rapidly climbing, as many of the ideas being developed are just now entering their commercial stages.
>
> 3. In addition to a 97% commercial success rate, virtually all (95%) of the positive projects developed by the businesses moved The Dow Chemical Company in the strategic directions desired by top management.

4. It is clear from the above analysis that it is possible to virtually eliminate major mistakes in new product development, while simultaneously developing substantial numbers of commercially profitable new products that fit the company's strategy. The projects identified as winners virtually all won.

This exceptional result at Dow is, of course, not a result only of Planned Innovation. The Dow Chemical Company is an excellent firm in every respect—management, personnel, and facilities. Planned Innovation was especially helpful in providing improved guidance and direction at the "fuzzy" front end of an existing development and commercialization process, including determining total product requirements early in the process. This example illustrates that Planned Innovation can help even sophisticated firms with existing new product development processes.

Example #2: Achieving Accelerated, Sustained Growth

Our objective from the beginning has been to develop a philosophy and process that will produce continuous successes, year in and year out, without the high cost of major failures. The net result of such a process is to produce steady growth in sales and profits through new product innovation.

The Donnelly Corporation, a medium-size firm headquartered in Holland, Michigan, is an international supplier of high-quality parts and component systems, mainly rear view mirrors, window systems, interior lighting, and trim systems. The Donnelly management was one of the earliest to embrace the Planned Innovation philosophy. The steady growth achieved by the firm over the 1985–95 decade, shown in Figure 1, was directly related to the use of Planned Innovation procedures.[3]

Rich Cook (who is now president of Cascade Engineering in Grand Rapids, Michigan) was formerly involved with much of this new product development activity at Donnelly.

As a young physicist working for Donnelly, learning this approach to marketing and product creation was a life-transforming experience. This training enabled me, working with the other team members at

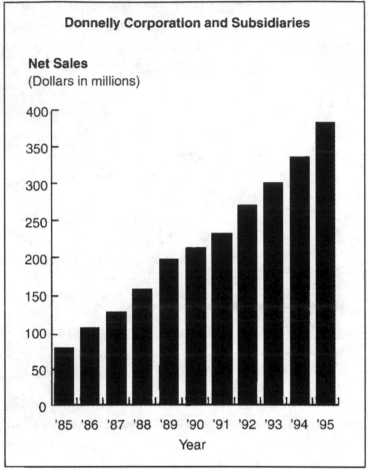

Donnelly Corporation and Subsidiaries

Net Sales
(Dollars in millions)

Figure 1

Donnelly, to create the first glass moonroof/sunroof for Ford Motor
Company and the "opera lite," a small decorative window for the Mark
and Lincoln Continental. The profitability of the glass moonroof pre-
vented significant job loss at Donnelly during the first oil shock. The
opera lite decorative window turned out to be the immediate precursor
of the automotive modular window.

Using the principles of Planned Innovation, many significant and innovative products were rapidly created over a decade. These included:
(1) coated glass for LCD displays used in consumer electronics such as
computers, watches, gas pumps, and clocks; (2) most of the computer
touch panels used in the U.S.; (3) the new lighted rear view mirror used
in cars, leading to totally new interior lighting in cars, enhancing the

safety, comfort, and convenience of all occupants; and, finally, (4) the new large-area, electrochromic mirror for heavy-duty trucks, which will improve long-haul trucking considerably.

In summary, the experience with Planned Innovation has affected the company over the past 20 years in a very positive manner, with the immediate or derivative products creating well over half of all the good-paying jobs at Donnelly today, the vast majority remaining in Western Michigan.

Example #3: Growth Through Improvements in Existing Products

Anyone who has witnessed recent Olympics gymnastics events or has watched them on television has seen the tangible benefits of Planned Innovation in action. Over the past twenty years, virtually every item of gymnastics equipment used there, from floor mats to high bars, was redesigned and improved by American Athletic, Inc. (AAI), of Jefferson, Iowa, using Planned Innovation principles. The net result is explained by Bill W. Sorenson, former president of AAI and now chairman of the parent company, American Sports Products Group, Inc., of White Plains, New York:

> American Athletic has made many significant engineering, design, material, and performance improvements in their gymnastics equipment over the past 20 years in a sport that for a long time was dominated by Eastern European countries. By following the principles of your Planned Innovation program, they became the world leader in new product innovations and the most respected international manufacturer of equipment for the sport of gymnastics.
>
> It is significant that the world-governing body for gymnastics, the Federal Internationale de Gymnastique (FIG), quickly adopted these innovations into their official apparatus technical specifications, and the higher level of performance provided to U.S. gymnasts by American's technically superior apparatus played a significant part in lifting U.S. gymnasts and gymnastics to world prominence.
>
> All of the equipment innovations and new products and designs added value to American's products. It not only enabled the company to

dominate its domestic market, but also to penetrate major overseas markets that would not have opened to them without superior equipment.

But the acid test is always profitability. As a direct result of its successful product development and marketing programs, American's gross profits on its gymnastics equipment increased more than 25%. This is a very significant profit improvement in a mature market like gymnastics.

Seeking ways to grow a stagnant small business unit, Planned Innovation procedures led to dramatic growth in sales and profits by replacing every existing product item in the gym with a better product. This was made possible by more objective, in-depth understanding of unmet customer needs, provided by our procedures.

In seeking to renew the growth and profitability of any business, we always start with reexamination of what might be done to address unmet needs in existing product-markets through modifications and extensions of existing products. Very often, this approach is the least expensive, fastest, and lowest-risk alternative to increased sales and profits. Planned Innovation procedures are especially suited to address such situations, because our approach is designed to achieve a depth of understanding that goes beyond the customers' understanding of their own unmet needs.

Example #4: Providing Guidance to R & D

Often central research units of large firms such as AMF or Dow Chemical, and in smaller companies as well, are essentially left on their own to decide which research projects would be in the best interest of the company. This usually results in a "technology-push" approach, where new technology is generated and then set off "looking for a home," which unfortunately is often not found.

Alternatively, central R & D groups are often asked to develop new products, without clear specifications of requirements, which often results in products which don't meet requirements when introduced to the market.

Both approaches have inefficiencies built in, because the proper level of market-based input is not provided to the researchers. And both approaches often frustrate researchers, who inherently want to contribute to successful outcomes.

We found that this critical communications gap could be effectively bridged in both of these firms, and in others as well, by cross-training a select few scientists and engineers as opportunity analysts, as part of a total Planned Innovation program. Dr. Clive P. Bosnyak, senior associate scientist at Dow, describes the result.

> The task was to identify value growth areas for high performance polymers so that research management could more effectively focus resources or, more likely, so they thought, find a home for all the technology we had on hand. Three months later, I had made little progress, but then came Planned Innovation.
>
> My first impression of Planned Innovation was the clear logic that was brought to the marketing and new product development process. Before then, the successful market or new product manager appeared to me to be a magician highly skilled in a mysterious art with secrets impervious to scientists and engineers.
>
> The ability for a scientist or engineer to be able to ask and understand questions related to the determination of business value creates strong links to the business people. In many industrial companies, there are increasing efforts to bridge the technical and business communities, and those people having Planned Innovation training have a strong competitive advantage in their career progressions. For engineers and scientists, the proper identification of market need focuses their programs; for marketing people, the tools dispel technical myths and fantasies. Perhaps, those people with Planned Innovation training appear to be the marketing magicians!

Would Planned Innovation Have Value to Your Firm?

Reflect for a moment on what the above four examples might suggest for your own firm. First, what would be the value of a ninety-plus percent success rate in new products, without the high costs of major failures? Think beyond the financial rewards to the synergistic effect on the firm's total productivity, resulting from the improved morale and heightened confidence an organization experiences from achieving success after success, with the necessary knowledge of a system to allow it to continue to do so.

Even if your firm has a functioning new product development process, how might surer guidance through the first two or three front-end steps dramatically improve the success of the total process? Our experience to date has been that the front end remains a weakness in the product development systems of practically every firm , and almost always can be improved with the Planned Innovation procedures.

Second, what value would your firm derive from a new product development process that essentially guarantees sustained growth through new products, year in and out, again without suffering the high costs of major failures?

Third, consider the value of creatively exhausting all the "near-in" opportunities available from modifying existing products for familiar existing markets, and extending their product life cycles—all accomplished with minimal cost, time, and risk.

Fourth, consider the value of the future efforts of your R & D personnel which have been wasted in the past because of lack of clear market guidance.

If you conclude that the Planned Innovation system might be of considerable value to your firm, read on to learn what it is and how it is done.

2

What Is Planned Innovation?

Planned Innovation is NOT another planning process. It is an action-oriented, practical, results-producing philosophy and process for achieving growth and profits through new product innovation. True, some important planning is required, such as a pilot does in planning a flight in an aircraft, but this planning must be followed by executing a disciplined sequence of flight procedures in order to reach an intended destination safely—every time.

There are many appropriate analogies between our philosophy and procedures and that of professional commercial airline operations. The chief executive of a firm which uses Planned Innovation is somewhat like the captain of a sophisticated airliner.

In the first place, airline captains don't allow the plane to take off until they know where they are going (target market), and until they have made certain that proper preflight planning has been done, including knowing that the plane has enough fuel (resources) to reach both the intended destination (new product) and the alternative destination, if unable to land at the intended one. The captain knows that the aircraft and crew can navigate and land at their destination, even among cloudy and foggy uncertainties (of undefined market needs and expanding technical alternatives) because they are following a series of well-rehearsed, disciplined procedures. They do not proceed "by the seat of their pants" on "a wing and a prayer." They approach their task seriously and professionally, recognizing that the lives of many passengers (stockholders' investment dollars) depend on the successful outcome of the flight (new product development). Under these conditions, you would expect a high percentage of successful trips (products) and very few failures, as is characteristic of commercial air travel today (and Planned Innovation).

Recall that it was not many decades ago that many doubted that reliable instrument flying would become an everyday reality. So it has been with our work in new product innovation. Many have doubted that any philosophy or method could produce success after success without major failures.

Another useful analogy is that adding Planned Innovation to a stagnant or slowly growing firm can be like adding a dynamic forward-passing offense to a football team which has historically used only a "three yards and a cloud of dust" ground-game offense. In referring to the impact of the forward pass 15 years after its introduction to the game, Elmer Berry, former head coach of football at YMCA College in Springfield, Massachusetts, noted, "It has taken away the advantage of numbers, weight, and power, and made the game one of brains, speed, and strategy."[4] Like the forward pass, our Planned Innovation procedures can start a company growing again, after all the downsizing, re-engineering, and total quality programs that have been the focus in recent years.

Our goal has been to discover why new product innovation has historically experienced such a high failure rate and to learn what can be done to prevent failure and assure success. Based on results of many studies, and our own experience as new product development engineers, we have directed our attention toward:

1. better defining product requirements to meet customer needs;
2. seeking ways to assure commercial success, rather than merely technical success; and
3. finding ways to collect and analyze appropriate information and coordinate activities across multi-functional boundaries.

We have found it useful to distinguish between invention and innovation, as shown in Figure 2. The distinction immediately places

---

What Is Innovation?

* INVENTION = Solution to a problem (unmet needs)
* INNOVATION = Commercially successful use of the invention
* PLANNED INNOVATION = Planned commercially successful use of solution to unmet needs

---

Figure 2

the focus on the ultimate objective (commercial success) rather than the intermediate objective (invention). It also provides an oversimplified but useful definition of Planned Innovation.

The Planned Innovation process starts with the mission and goals of each individual firm and major business units within the firm, and then converts these objectives to tangible opportunity selection criteria to proactively guide the search and selection of opportunities. Planned Innovation uses an efficient, scientific reasoning process to evaluate and shape the development of each product or service to meet identified customer needs of sufficient value (to the customer) in a way that produces the desired growth in sales and profits for the firm.

Thus, in a logical, practical way, Planned Innovation spans and provides necessary linkages from strategic plans to tactical action plans involving new products needed to implement long-range objectives.

Our philosophy of approach to new products is based on the premise that, in essence, all new product innovation involves two basic functions: the identification and capturing of value. These two functions can be accomplished by a variety of methods or processes ranging from accidental discoveries to systematically planned research. Most new product activities probably involve a mix of both art and science, some relying more heavily on art and others on science.

Our method reflects more of a scientific than an arts approach, because only with the power of a scientific approach can a firm reliably predict future product requirements beyond the customer's knowledge with the understanding needed to cope with the changing technological and market environment. While we recognize the importance of stimulating and nourishing a creative spark in any successful new product process, our objective is to provide a means for accomplishing all necessary activities in a systematic and efficient way that any firm can learn to use.

Our view is that all value is basically derived from a combination of (1) meeting unmet functional needs in target markets and (2) meeting existing needs better or more economically. Value is captured, after identifying such needs, by developing appropriate physical and non-physical products, and associated production and marketing plans to serve identified target markets.

We thus place great stress on the identification of unmet needs and the associated value to customers in specific target markets. We have continually developed and refined techniques for determining product requirements, especially where the unmet need and potential solutions go beyond the understanding of the customer.

We also emphasize that value can be effectively captured only if the total requirements are within the domain of resources of the firm, or its ability to obtain and manage any additional resources required. We further hold that all new product innovation activity should fall within an overall business strategy of the firm and that successive new products should build synergistically toward the implementation of long-range business objectives. To aid in achieving these purposes, we believe that new product selection criteria should be framed in a way which proactively guides the search for new products and assures that a good matching of resources to opportunities will be achieved.

Like instrument flying, Planned Innovation requires a combination of ingredients and techniques, all quite straightforward on their own, but blended together in a unique and very exact way to achieve the right results.

3

The Planned Innovation System

Planned Innovation is a workable combination of philosophy and procedure, a very real way of identifying and shaping the development of potential opportunities. A one-sentence definition is not possible; instead, the interrelated parts form a whole system, as presented in Figure 3. Note that the system is for achieving *continuous success in new product innovation without major failures.* Despite the desirability (and attainability) of continuous success, some minor failures are to be expected because of the experimental nature of research activities involved. It is only the major failures that are to be avoided, with the accompanying large costs caused by misdirected investments and the lost time and efforts of personnel involved.

Looking at the whole system might at first seem overwhelming. But once you understand the pieces, the puzzle will fit together perfectly—and the system will help you look at decision making in an entirely new way. Each of the system's five elements, outlined here, will be explored in depth as the rest of this book unfolds.

Element One: A Disciplined Scientific Reasoning Process

In no activity in business is there greater value for a disciplined scientific thought process than in new product innovation. This is true

---

The Planned Innovation System

**(For Continuous Success in New Product
Innovations Without Major Failures)**

1.   Use a disciplined scientific reasoning process throughout all managerial levels and functions involved.

2.   Ensure lasting market orientation for existing and new business.

3.   Ensure identification and selection of appropriate new opportunities (for evaluation) by proactively using opportunity selection criteria that reflect:

 a.   Both strategic and tactical business objectives and financial goals.
 b.   Dynamic matching of resources to present and future opportunities.
 c.   Positive and negative influences of major external trends affecting present and future business opportunities.

4.   Evaluate and guide development of opportunities by determining critical requirements for success with sufficient depth and precision prior to major expenditures by using scientific reasoning process together with the Planned Innovation Models to provide discipline and structure and unambiguous communications among diverse functions.

5.   Ensure creative multifunctional involvement throughout the development process.

Figure 3

for all levels of management and all functions. People with different positions, backgrounds, and training must communicate clearly and understand each other while engaged in cross-functional problem-solving in a changing environment characterized by many unknowns and risks.

The need for disciplined scientific reasoning is greatest when developing a completely new product for a new, unfamiliar market. The unknowns are greatest in this case, as is the risk of failure. It reminds us, as active pilots, of the same situation as that of flying a new aircraft to an unfamiliar destination airport in bad weather conditions, making an instrument approach to the minimum allowed altitude and visibility. Needless to say, we had better be well trained with sharp skills, but, moreover, we had better be *disciplined* in flight procedures, use of checklists, and cockpit crew coordination, using precise, unambiguous communication. When flight conditions become tough, as described above, it is the discipline in use of checklists, procedures, and clear communication among crew members that is paramount for a safe flight. Training and experience are, of course, valuable, but it is discipline that keeps you out of trouble. After all, if conditions become too extreme, it is discipline that says we had better turn around or go to an alternate airport with better ceilings and visibility.

A similar analogy is also useful concerning minor modifications and extensions of existing products for existing markets. In this situation, there are few unknowns and the risk of failure is minimal—analogous to taking a short hop in a familiar airplane to a familiar airport on a calm, sunny day. A piece of cake! Yet, if you observed a professional airline crew on such a trip, you'd see them go through all the same checklists (maybe a little quicker), using the same disciplined procedures described in the first example. What some people may not realize is that it is the disciplined repetition of the proven procedures that *assures* that the flight will be a piece of cake, and the process doesn't take any longer! Furthermore, if any unexpected events occurred, like a deer or vehicle suddenly appearing on the runway (or a competing product just introduced), the crew will be alert and ready to take appropriate action.

The use of a disciplined scientific reasoning process gives maximum protection against failure *and* maximum assurance of success, usually at no extra time or cost. Because of the value of such a disciplined thought process in new product development, we have devised appropriate models and associated procedures to reinforce this process in every aspect of the system.

Element Two: Lasting Market Orientation

The product innovation activities of a business are greatly enhanced by the adoption of a market orientation, in contrast to a production or sales orientation. The basic idea is not new. A market orientation means that all business activities are focused on meeting the needs of customers in identified market segments. On the other hand, a production or sales orientation means that the focus of activity is on producing and selling certain products with little or no emphasis on meeting needs of customers in specified segments.

However, the significance of a true market orientation is often overlooked in business. When integrated into all business functions, a market orientation assures that all changes in products, whether modifications in existing products or new products, will only be done to meet an identified market need that a customer has, one that the firm can address and make a suitable profit in doing so.

In essence, becoming market-oriented is the first (and minimal) step needed throughout a business organization to provide a disciplined reasoning process. Interestingly, although many firms profess to be market-oriented, we have found very few firms in industrial/commercial and aerospace/defense markets which have internalized the concept well enough to realize the best possible benefits to new product innovation activities.

Unfortunately, becoming market-oriented is not something that comes easily or naturally to most businesses. It seems much more natural to focus on "what we know how to produce" or "what we have in stock to sell." Consequently, after firms make the conscious effort to a market orientation, it is easy to "backslide" into a sales or production orientation.

That's why we emphasize the importance of a *lasting* market orientation. The longer and more ingrained the orientation becomes within the corporate culture, the more assured the benefits, and the more efficient (and successful) the new product development process becomes.

Element Three: Proper Selection Criteria

To be effective, new product selection criteria must be developed thoughtfully to reflect management consensus concerning a number of factors. These factors include the strategic direction of the business, together with financial goals and tactical objectives toward which the new products are expected to advance the business. The selection criteria must also identify the major capabilities and strengths, and basis for competitive openings and advantage, on which new products should build. The criteria must identify the external trends, both positive and negative, which will likely affect existing and new business.

When truly representative of these factors, such criteria can be used with confidence to quickly prioritize opportunities on a continuous basis so that the best ones are always being developed. It is important to realize that such criteria can do much more than prioritize existing opportunities. The same criteria also can be used in a proactive manner to suggest the type of products that would advance the business toward its objectives. Used in this manner, a properly constructed set of criteria can focus the selective perception of many persons in the organization (especially in marketing and R & D) to be looking constantly for the "right kind" of new product opportunities.

It should be noted that this procedure for prioritizing opportunities is only the first step in an evaluation process, not the total evaluation. Nevertheless, conscientious use of such criteria can have a major impact on the overall effectiveness of a new product development program by keeping it focused on opportunities which will have greatest value, both tactically and strategically.

Element Four: Using Scientific Reasoning to Determine Requirements Before Making Major Expenditures

If it were possible to determine the total requirements for a new product prior to major expenditures and thereby accelerate the process and give needed guidance with minimal risk, why wouldn't firms always want to do so? They certainly would, but we have found there have been two major obstacles that have often blocked the process. First, there were no comprehensive models which could be easily understood and applied to any and all types of new product innovation. Our models of requirements for successful innovation and bases of value were developed for this purpose and refined through application to provide practical answers to this universal need.

Second, the procedures for determining requirements were either too costly, too time-consuming, too imprecise, or all of the above. We have addressed this problem by devising sequential, small-sample scientific procedures to be used with the models. This makes it possible to determine quickly and efficiently all critical requirements early in the development process with sufficient depth and precision to guide technical, manufacturing, and marketing developments.

The scientific procedures actually provide discipline to the entire evaluation process, including determination of requirements. An important byproduct is precision in definition of terms, requirements, and issues to be resolved, providing unambiguous communication among the various functions involved. The improved understanding among all functions enhances the confidence among participants and speeds the entire process.

Element Five: Ensure Multifunctional Involvement

As we have helped establish our Planned Innovation procedures in many different firms with almost every conceivable organizational structure and culture, we learned that the key to swift, successful new product innovation is to achieve appropriate multifunctional involvement at every step in the process. The advantages are enormous. It helps achieve fast, clear communication of problems and requirements to all functions, leading to the focusing of the best talent available to understand and solve problems, and making it possible to proceed with parallel actions across functions as soon as requirements are identified. The key in all cases is to be certain that target market segments and their needs and value are defined with adequate precision to provide appropriate input to the technical, manufacturing, and marketing functions.

When all five elements of the system are established and made operational, continuous success in new product innovation is virtually assured, because if success cannot be achieved, the project is either terminated quickly (before major expenditures are made) or modified to assure success.

4

Establishing a Disciplined Scientific Reasoning Process for New Product Innovation

Most businesses operate with a disciplined thought process in finance, accounting, manufacturing, engineering and research, and in legal matters. Unfortunately, the functions where disciplined reasoning processes are frequently not used are those that affect new product innovation the most. These include managerial strategic planning and direction, marketing and sales, and, to some extent, organization and staffing.

There is an important distinction to be made between a disciplined thought process alone and a scientific disciplined thought process. It is possible to be disciplined in thought in the sense that one is consistent in behavior, without basing such thought consciously on any well-structured models. A disciplined scientific thought process is based on appropriate models or structures to guide the reasoning process. It is a scientific disciplined thought process that leads to consistent success in new product innovation.

We have observed that those business functions where more disciplined thought processes prevail are also those with more objective standards, logical structures, models, or, if you will, laws of man or nature to guide everyday decision making. In essence, a quasi-scientific disciplined reasoning process also prevails. For example, financial and cost accounting procedures are generally well defined and understood, as are manufacturing procedures and standards, and technical research and engineering design activities. All have well-defined models or structures on which to base reasoning.

However, insofar as new product innovation is concerned, there has not been the same degree of practical, well-defined structures, models, and associated procedures to guide management thought processes, and to help integrate the activities of diverse functional departments.

Engineers and scientists working in the physical and biological sciences routinely develop models of a phenomenon under investigation to guide their research. An architect may build a small-scale physical model of a bridge or other structure. An aircraft designer may build a scale model of an airplane for wind tunnel testing. More recently, computers have made it possible (and economically feasible) to construct mathematical models of structures using the technique of finite element analysis for application in designing aircraft, boats, and automobiles. Computer simulation has also expanded the usefulness of statistical models of phenomena such as highway traffic and aircraft arrivals to a busy terminal to aid in the design of roads and airports.

Additionally, models which classify items or objects and depict relationships, such as characteristics of birds or animals and the periodic table of elements, can nevertheless be useful in guiding inquiry in a disciplined fashion. In this way, one of the simplest structured, descriptive models used in marketing, such as McCarthy's 4 P's Model of Components of a Marketing Strategy, can be extremely valuable in analyzing whether a certain marketing strategy is complete or whether a better one can be devised.[5]

Regardless of the method of construction, whether physical, mathematical, pictorial, or organized lists of words or concepts, all models form the basis for reasoning. In the same sense, the structured checklists used by aircraft pilots are models which provide a basis for their reasoning. This is especially true of the checklists for handling aircraft emergencies which guide the pilots' thought processes as they diagnose a problem, such as an engine out or landing gear failure, all while they are also flying the aircraft.

In actuality, each manager's past experience is also a model from which they reason, which may be very adequate for operating in a well-known existing business. Herein lies a major problem for successful innovation. If any major aspect of the new product development activity extends *beyond* the experience (model) of the managers involved, they have a limited basis for decision-making. This can happen if the new product requires dramatically new technology in design or manufacture. It is a problem especially when an entirely new market is also involved.

This explains why the frequent policy of "sticking to one's own knitting" often makes a lot of sense. As long as the only changes required in product-market strategies are minor modifications in existing products for existing customers, then the past experience of the management team may be an adequate model. But what should be done when competition develops a *new* material or product that is destined to make an existing product obsolete or when the customer's need changes so that modification of an existing product is not enough? A guidance system is needed that can lead a firm unerringly into new product territory—in essence, an instrument navigation system, complete with weather radar to avoid thunderstorms.

It was with this end in mind that we developed the fundamental Planned Innovation model describing the total requirements for success in innovation, and devised procedures for using it. In addition, we developed the Basis of Value model for identifying sources of value, which are components of the fundamental model. We also found that other model-like frameworks and constructs were also needed to fully define and implement the entire process. Much is involved, starting with giving initial direction, identifying appropriate opportunities, prioritizing among alternatives, evaluating them, determining all requirements with sufficient precision (product, economic, technical, manufacturing, marketing, and competitive), and, finally, guiding and coordinating cross-functional development activities.

Our overall objective has been to provide models with associated procedures which will allow businesses to predict with understanding all requirements for successful innovation. It is the ability to predict with understanding that philosopher of science Stephen Toulmin has shown to be an appropriate general aim of science, defined in Figure 4.[6]

Scientific Method

- The general aim of science is to predict with understanding.

- Our aim is to *predict* what will be required for an existing or new business to reach our sales and profit objectives together with the *understanding* of why it will or will not happen.

Figure 4

The view that the general aim of science is to predict with under-standing is particularly appropriate as the basis for reasoning in all phases of new product innovation activity. First, firms must deter-mine (predict) what types of opportunities are appropriate given an understanding of the strategic and tactical objectives, and strengths and weaknesses, versus their competition. Then they must predict, among opportunities identified, which are more likely to succeed, again based on appropriate understanding of why or why not. Every step in the evaluation process and determining of diverse multifunctional requirements is a process of predicting what the re-quirements are, again with understanding of why those and not oth-ers are the requirements.

It is the combination of appropriate accuracy and precision in prediction with the associated total understanding of the reasons be-hind the prediction that produces the power in science and its use-fulness in new product innovation. Prediction alone is not enough.

Stephen Toulmin illustrated this by pointing out that between 600 and 400 B.C. the Babylonians' arithmetic techniques enabled them to forecast the first visibility of the new moon and lunar eclipse with great accuracy, and extend the calculations to predict the move-ments of major planets. Yet they did it without any theoretical basis (understanding) as to the physical nature of the heavenly bodies. Any method of prediction of any phenomenon, even though accu-rate, without an accompanying understanding is a setup for impend-ing disaster. History has also recorded the failures of the Babylonian wise men who tried to use the same mathematical techniques to pre-dict earthquakes and plagues of locusts.[7]

Consider an extension of this example to the present. The same arithmetical skill in forecasting the movement of the planets might have some use in the initial launch of a space shuttle. The arithmetical, skill might help time the launch correctly and provide initial guidance. But, without our present knowledge (understanding) of astrophysics, the shuttle's guidance computers could not calculate the mid-course and final-course corrections to reach its destination.

Every new product innovation is like a space shuttle mission. The initial launch (opportunity identification and prioritization) needs to have correct general guidance, but as the evaluation process continues and multifunctional requirements are determined in greater and greater detail, there are many mid- and final-course corrections that typically must be done, with understanding, to predict correctly the many things that will ensure ultimate success in the market. Although there is some debate about what constitutes science, we have found that the concept of scientific process shown in Figure 5 to be acceptable and practical.

Scientific process starts with a model or theoretical framework as the basis for reasoning (or research). The model used should be appropriate for the situation being analyzed. It might be the product life cycle model when determining appropriate marketing strategy. We use the two Planned Innovation models we developed when evaluating new opportunities, but we often use other models to as-

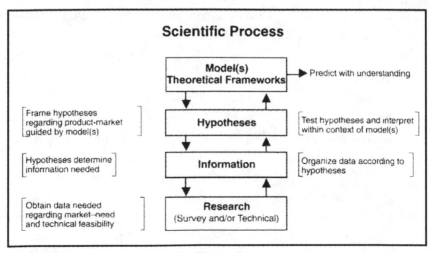

Figure 5

sist with the total analysis process. The descending arrows on the left side of the boxes in Figure 5 indicate that hypotheses are framed concerning the product-market opportunity based on the model. The hypotheses themselves suggest what information is needed in order to accept or reject them.

The term *hypothesis* often sounds theoretical, academic, and nonpractical to businessmen and women when they first hear it. They are not used to verbalizing their thoughts as hypotheses, much less writing them down. However, in learning the discipline, they find it much like learning to ride a bicycle—awkward at first, but soon second nature.

The research activity required depends on the type of information needed. It is conceivable that, if the opportunity being considered involves only a minor modification to an existing product for an existing market, almost all the needed information would be already available within the firm. On the other hand, just the opposite would most likely be true if a new product for a new market were being considered.

After the research activity has been completed, the reasoning process would proceed as shown by the ascending arrows on the right side of the boxes in the figure. The data would be organized and analyzed to test the hypotheses, and the results would be interpreted within the context of the model to predict requirements with understanding based on the total process—the validity of the model, the hypotheses, the research method used, and the correct interpretation in terms of the model.

The entire process to evaluate an opportunity could be a description of an elaborate, well-documented research process or simply a disciplined mental exercise such as using a checklist to touch all bases. It might require strict adherence to the disciplined flight crew procedures using multiple checklists when conducting a flight in bad weather; or it could be a quick rundown of the checklists for a short flight in good weather. The important point is that it takes no greater time or effort to go through the scientific reasoning process whether you are considering an easy or difficult flight (opportunity). The process is always there to help out if things do not turn out as expected. An important result is that, after a while, the reasoning process really becomes second nature. Managers tell us that they can't imagine how they ever made decisions without it, and they would be very uncomfortable making any decisions without it after they have internalized the process. Our fundamental model depicting total requirements for successful innovation is easily memorized and internalized, along with our related model for identifying sources of value.

5

The Model of Requirements
for Successful Innovation

Our experience has shown that new product innovation is best accomplished by determining the critical requirements for success with sufficient depth and precision to guide development activities before major expenditures on technical research and design, and especially before major expenditures on manufacturing facilities and marketing and distribution efforts. The formulation of a complete, practical model to represent the total requirements for successful new product innovation and the development of associated procedures for its implementation have been our central focus for many years.

Our work in defining product requirements for large military and commercial systems led us to become familiar with mathematical modeling techniques of operations research and large-scale systems design, as well as computer simulation. Recognizing that every new product innovation is a complex, multidimensional solution to some problem, it was natural for us to try to formulate a model which described the situation and encompassed the three guiding tasks mentioned above.

Our first thought was that every new product innovation might be expressed as a simultaneous solution to a set of equations. If somehow each set of requirements could be expressed mathematically, then perhaps we could solve for a single solution.

On further reflection, we realized that very few new product solutions are actually unique. Usually there are several products, often embodying different technical approaches, which are alternative solutions to the same problem. A model that produced a single (point) solution was not the best depiction. Instead, a model that could result in multiple solutions would be a better alternative.

This reasoning led us to think of linear programming as the appropriate mathematical model. Such a model solves a set of inequalities (requirements) to produce not *one* solution, but a solution *space*. In the model, all solutions within the space are feasible products.

A second step is then required—to pick the best solution (product) within the solution space. This is done by evaluating the possibilities with an objective or optimizing function. The objective function could include only a single factor, such as Return on Investment (ROI), or multiple factors (ROI, Time, Total Money Invested, etc.).

Conceptually, a linear programming model appeared to be a good fit, although we recognized that the reduction of all factors to appropriate quantitative measures might be very difficult or impossible to accomplish. We realized also that the abstraction that would be required to quantify all variables might render a theoretically satisfying but practically unusable solution. Nevertheless, we felt the concept to be a useful construct on which to proceed.

It was with this concept of linear programming in mind that we formulated the Model of Requirements for Successful Innovation, which has been used successfully in hundreds of applications over the years. The basic domains of this model, shown in Figure 6, depict the total requirements for successful innovation as the simultaneous solution to requirements in five fundamentally different, but overlapping, domains.

1. Market Requirements
2. Functional (Product) Requirements
3. Economic Requirements
4. Resource Requirements
5. Competitive Requirements

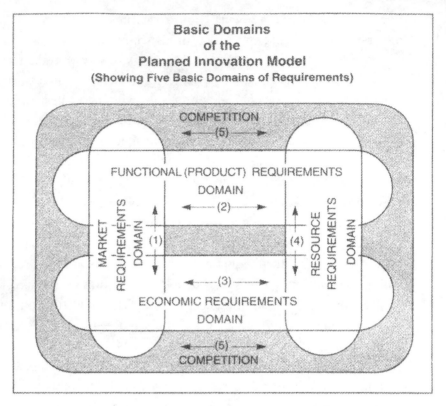

Figure 6

When using the five domains to evaluate a specific new product opportunity, the overlap in the domains provides the point of focus in determining the solution to the requirements. The overlapping corners of the five domains are shown in the complete model in Figure 7. The complete model identifies nine segments of focus.

1. Physical (product) functional need required in the market (such as computer hardware mainframe and accessories, etc.)
2. Nonphysical (product) functional need required in the target market (such as software, training, and service)
3. Economic value (source and amount) to the customer in the target market of meeting the physical and nonphysical functional needs
4. Emotive value (source and amount) to the customer in the tar-

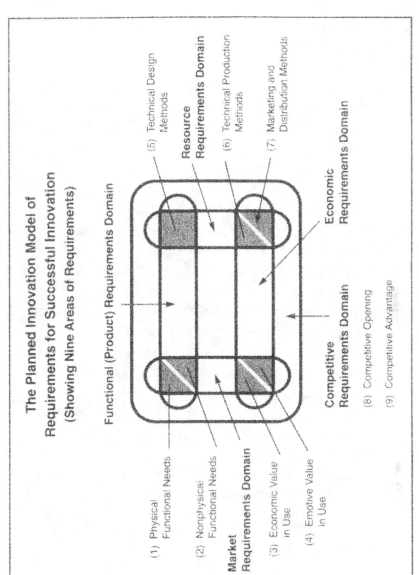

The Planned Innovation Model of Requirements for Successful Innovation (Showing Nine Areas of Requirements)

Functional (Product) Requirements Domain

(5) Technical Design Methods

Resource Requirements Domain

(6) Technical Production Methods

(7) Marketing and Distribution Methods

Economic Requirements Domain

Market Requirements Domain

(1) Physical Functional Needs

(2) Nonphysical Functional Needs

(3) Economic Value in Use

(4) Emotive Value in Use

Competitive Requirements Domain

(8) Competitive Opening

(9) Competitive Advantage

Figure 7

get market of meeting the physical and nonphysical functional needs

5. Technical resources (type and amount of technology, personnel, and facilities) required for the technical research, development, and product design which will meet the physical and
   nonphysical functional product requirements within the constraints of the product's total economic and emotive value to
   the customer in the target market

6. Manufacturing resources (type and amount of resources required to manufacture the product given the required technology, levels of quality and volumes, while constrained by the
   economics of value in use to the customer in the target market)

7. Marketing and distribution (methods, type, and amount of resources required)

8. Basis for competitive opening (which might occur for any
   number of reasons, such as a new technical discovery making
   it possible to satisfy an unmet need which cannot be met by
   any competitors, or the failure of a competitor's product to perform adequately)

9. Basis for competitive advantage (which may result from
   meeting the unmet need with a superior product providing
   greater value in use, protected by a group of patents in technical design or perhaps unique production technology and/or
   superiority in implementing one or more elements in the marketing strategy)

Note that our concept of a product is a broad construct that en-
compasses anything that meets the physical and nonphysical functional needs. Thus, the product can be (1) all physical, such as a
computer, machine tool, or fighter aircraft; (2) a combination of
physical and nonphysical functional needs, such as a computer system plus a training and service program; or (3) all nonphysical, such
as a cleaning, repair, or training service. Most nonphysical products
often do have some important functional needs for physical products such as cleaning supplies, repair tools and spare parts, and
training manuals needed to effectively deliver the dominant nonphysical portion of the total product.

In applying the model, the nine areas represent an organized checklist or framework to ensure that all areas are covered. However, most new product innovations do not require detailed analysis of every area before technical development can begin. **Almost always, the critical areas are analysis of unmet market need and associated value in use, and determination of basis for competitive opening and advantage.** If these critical requirements are well understood, it is often obvious whether or not the product can be successfully developed, manufactured, and marketed within the economic and other resource constraints. Because the identification and measurement of value in use is of critical importance in defining requirements, we developed a subsidiary model to assist with implementing that portion (items 3 and 4) of the fundamental model.

Model for Identifying Economic and Emotive Value

No concept is more central to the process of new product innovation than identifying value. From the perspective of a firm seeking successful new product innovation, there are two basic sources of value: (1) meeting unmet functional needs of customers in target markets, and (2) meeting existing needs better, or more economically.

Our approach is to identify the basis of value in terms of the unmet and/or met needs in specific target markets, and then to assess the magnitude or value to the customer of meeting the need(s). The value is captured by developing appropriate physical and nonphysical products which can be manufactured and marketed at a price consistent with both the value to the customers and the sales and profit objectives of the firm, additionally constrained by competitive offerings.

Our concept of sources of value is very close to the concept of entrepreneurship as defined by economist Israel Kirzner to be "the ability to detect opportunities (for profit) not seen by others."[8] Every business is founded on some degree of entrepreneurship which recognizes a potential value to a group of customers which the business can provide at a profit. Thus, successfully identifying and capturing value is also a logical result of a market orientation.

A number of theories of value have been advanced by economists during the past several centuries. Perhaps best known and understood is the labor theory of value, which states that the value of a product or service depends on the amount (value) of labor involved. The theory can be extended to recognize the contribution of capital as well.

Despite their logical validity, approaches from the supply side do not provide a practical basis for decisions by customers who have specific unmet needs to fill. Instead, new product development requires a market-side approach to a theory of value. In addressing this issue, we have found it conceptually useful to define value from the viewpoint of the user (or potential customer) in terms of the functions performed by a product in a given product-market. This places emphasis on what a product does for the customer, or what it permits the customer to do in defined target markets. The approach therefore gives recognition to the possibility that the same product may have different values to customers in different markets where the functions performed are essentially the same.

In order to identify value, you need to know what you are looking for and where it is likely to be found, to be constantly on the lookout for new opportunities. A given product usually performs several functions that provide value to the user. That value can be identified and analyzed in terms of its economic and emotive basis.

Economic value is financially based, and is therefore often described as *rational*. Economic value can result from cost savings, such as substituting one product (material, component part, machine, or service) for another or from an improved return on investment in one product (like a truck or machine tool) in comparison to another in use.

Emotive value is based on a human response to a sensory stimulus, which may involve any of the five senses—sight, sound, touch, taste, or smell. Emotive value can also result from a stimulus that produces a human psychological response such as joy, pride, esteem, love, or affection.

The concept of economic and emotive bases of value for any product is illustrated in Figure 8, where the economic and emotive elements of value, shown as weights, are on opposite ends of a scale like a playground teeter-totter.

For typical industrial/commercial products, the mixtures may vary from almost totally economic, such as a mix of ninety percent eco-

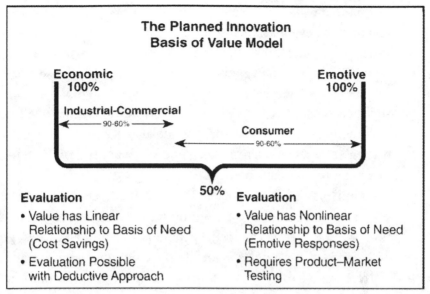

Figure 8

nomic and ten percent emotive (for standard supplies like cutting tool bits for machine tools), to a mix of sixty percent economic and forty percent emotive (for a new computer system or headquarters office building). Consumer products usually have larger components of emotive versus economic value. For example, clothing products may vary from a mix of almost totally emotive value, such as evening gowns and high-heeled shoes, to a mix of less emotive and more economic value for casual wear or work clothing, such as blue jeans for miners and cowboys. For some work clothing, the mix may even be more like an industrial/commercial product.

The initial objective in the assessment of new product opportunities is to recognize the presence of both bases of value, so that both may be taken into account in subsequent analysis. Different research procedures are needed to evaluate each, as indicated in the figure.

Economic value is generally linear in nature because it depends on cost savings, which generally can be evaluated with straightforward deductive cost analysis techniques. Such analysis can become complicated, however, when costs and benefits are not directly related, such as improved performance of military weapons or faster operating speed of the CPU of a new computer.

Emotive value, on the other hand, is generally nonlinear in nature and must be evaluated in a stimulus-response mode. For example, a little of a certain color applied to a product may hardly be noticed (and have little or no emotive value); a moderate intensity of color may be considered very attractive (adding emotive value); while a stronger intensity of the same color may be considered unattractive (subtracting emotive value). The value also depends on responses in particular target product-markets, and may vary widely from market to market for the same product.

Emotive value is a two-edged sword. It can be strongly positive or negative, depending on the cultural background of the market. For example, German nationals generally like the color forest green, whereas French nationals associate the color with the German Luftwaffe, seen too often during World War II. It would be unfortunate, therefore, if a major U.S. airplane manufacturer were to display a new aircraft at the Paris air show, directed toward the French market, painted Luftwaffe green!

While manufacturers of consumer products are usually tuned to the positive and negative value of the emotive elements, and design their products accordingly, industrial/commercial and military product manufacturers often are not. There is much to be gained from understanding the emotive factors associated with any product.

For example, wiring harnesses for aircraft jet engines require high reliability and long life, while facilitating easy maintenance of the entire engine. The high reliability and long life provide the main source of value—as any return on investment over time (thus, an economically based source of value). One manufacturer was able to provide an additional significant component of emotive value as well, by choosing a pattern of brightly colored wires in the harnesses, giving the engine an overall image of aesthetic beauty. True, the different colors made it easy to trace the leads when working on the engines, but that (economic) function could also be done by the black, gray, and white wires used by the major competitors. The bright blues, yellows, and reds in the harnesses did much more. They transformed a dull gray machine into a thing of vibrant beauty, appreciated by everyone who saw it, especially engineers and mechanics. Mechanics even commented that it lifted their spirits every time they removed the cowling from an engine for maintenance.

It should not be surprising to learn that the firm that used the brightly colored wires became the vendor of choice, even at a premium price, because the colorful harness provided greater *total* value when both economic and emotive components were considered.

Identifying customer needs in target markets, and determining the presence and magnitude of both economic and emotive sources of value, are central to determining requirements for successful new product innovation.

How the Models are Used

The fundamental model of total requirements shown in Figure 7, and the subsidiary model of bases of value (Figure 8) provide the framework for reasoning on which hypotheses are formed which starts the whole analysis process leading to predicting total requirements with the understanding necessary to new product innovation.

When requirements for a given new product innovation are specified in all nine areas of focus, we have the operational equivalent to the simultaneous solution to a set of nine inequalities. This defines a solution space of requirements for a new product. Any product that meets the total requirements in all nine areas would fall within the solution space, and could be a successful solution (product). Although we have not achieved a truly mathematical representation of the model, the conceptual framework has proven to be very valuable in developing research procedures to determine requirements quickly and efficiently.

Four Questions to Address in Each Segment of Focus

The essential information required to define all requirements for a given product-market can be obtained by addressing each of the nine segments of focus in the model with the four framework questions shown in Figure 9.

When these four questions are applied to the nine areas of focus in the model, a matrix of information requirements is defined as

---

**Four Framework Questions Used
in Determining New Product Requirements**

1. How is the basic function performed now (for which the new product
   or service is expected to provide improvement)?

2. What does the present method cost?

3. What is wrong with the present method (and what improvement is
   needed in present methods)?

4. What value would the improvements have (to the intended user)?

Figure 9

shown in schematic form in Figure 10. The matrix of information
shown in this Figure is designed to translate the abstract conceptual
model of requirements into "real world" items of information that
provide the depth of understanding and detail necessary to specify
actual requirements for a given product-market.

Certainly not all the information is needed before the development can proceed. Although the matrix provides a comprehensive
outline of information needed, obtaining all the information is a
complex and time-consuming series of tasks. We have spent years
learning just what information is needed at each stage in the assessment process, and how to obtain that information quickly, efficiently, and with sufficient precision and accuracy to proceed
confidently without fear of major error.

Opportunity Selection Criteria Become the Optimizing Function

Once several possible solutions have been defined that meet the
total product requirements, the firm must decide which is the best
solution. A choice needs to be made among several possible opportunities, giving rise to the need to screen or prioritize the alternatives. Now, though, the total requirements have been determined in
much greater detail than in the initial selection process.

Therefore, the best solution for a given firm is that which best fits

Matrix of Information Requirements
(for Each Product–Market)

Four Questions:

Areas of Focus within Model:	1 How is basic function performed now?	2 What does present method cost?	3 What is wrong with present method?	4 What value would improvements have?
1. Physical (Product) Functional Need				
2. Nonphysical Functional Need				
3. Economic Value (in Use)				
4. Emotive Value (in Use)				
5. Technical Design and Development				
6. Technical Production/ Process Methods				
7. Marketing and Distribution Methods				
8. Competitive Opening (Basis)				
9. Competitive Advantage (Basis)				

Figure 10

the specific criteria previously established by that firm. The optimizing function (in the sense of a linear programming model) is composed of both quantitative and qualitative criteria. The specific criteria ensure that the opportunity will contribute toward meeting the firm's strategic and tactical objectives, will constitute a proper matching of resources compared to competition in the product-market to be addressed, and will be in consonance with long-run external trends without bucking any. The preferred (or best) solution depends on both quantitative projections of sales, costs, and profits, and qualitative judgments among choices of technology, manufacturing, and marketing methods. Often these qualitative judgments are based on the best matching of total resources to the requirements of the opportunity, and on which alternatives will produce the strongest and most durable competitive advantages.

6

Forming a Lasting
Market Orientation

The fact that a true market orientation is desirable and of value for any business is widely accepted today. After all, the concept has been around since the 1950s. If you ask members of almost any management team if they agree with the concept, the answer will be an immediate and definite "yes." Yet, if you press them for a clear and precise definition of the term, and ask further why that orientation is more valuable than others, you will likely get answers like, "I've always heard that is true," or "That's what you marketing professors taught us was the best way." In truth, we have usually found widespread lip-service agreement, but infrequent, incomplete integration of the concept throughout the business, especially in marketing plans and new product development activities.

Definition of Business Orientations

Recall the salient characteristics of the classic business orientations shown in Figure 11.

A production orientation is so termed because the entire business focus is on producing a certain product with little or no em-

---

Business Orientations

Production orientation
- Focuses on: What we can make.
- Deemphasizes: Meeting customer needs.

Sales orientation
- Focuses on: Pushing what we've got.
- Deemphasizes: Meeting customer needs through product innovation.

Market Orientation
- Focuses on: Meeting customer needs.
- Requires: (1) Precise definition of target markets.
                                 (2) Detailed understanding of customer needs.
- Results in: (1) All business functions oriented toward serving customers.
                                 (2) Above average long-run profit.

Figure 11

phasis on understanding customer needs, or creative use of marketing and advertising. The focus implicitly reflects a situation where customers' unmet need are so basic and strong that they will seek out the firm producing the product, come to the factory, and purchase it.

A sales orientation is similar to a production orientation in that the firm does not place emphasis on meeting customer needs, but attempts to sell or "push" existing products to customers through use of effective sales promotion and advertising. In essence, it tries to reach out to customers and convince them to buy the existing, on-the-shelf, products.

The market orientation, shown last in the figure, differs from the first two in several ways, but most significantly by its central focus on meeting customer needs. To achieve this focus, firms must define their target markets precisely and obtain a detailed understanding of customer needs (and the value of meeting those needs). This focus both requires and, ultimately, results in all business functions (R & D, manufacturing, and finance, as well as marketing) becoming oriented toward meeting customer needs. And, when the market orientation is well implemented, it can result in an above average long-run profit, as the following example illustrates.

Blue Jeans—A Universal Example

Almost every manager in every major firm worldwide is familiar with blue jeans, and has heard the story of the development of blue jeans by Levi Strauss, Inc., during the California gold rush in the 1860s.

Thousands of fortune seekers pouring into California soon learned that mining and panning for gold was hard on clothes, especially pants, and sought desirable replacements for those quickly wearing out. Levi Strauss recognized the unmet need, and created a new durable product made of a blue denim material that had been imported from southern France.

What business orientation would have been appropriate for Levi Strauss during those times? It is easy to visualize that a production orientation would have made good sense. The major management problem centered on obtaining enough material, sewing machines, and skilled labor to produce blue jeans as fast as possible. The unmet need was so basic and universal that minimal product requirements research would have been required. The need was so strong that only a few sizes were needed. Any size that would fit approximately would have done, as long as it was big enough to be held up with a belt and long enough to turn up at the cuff, if necessary. Very little marketing would have been necessary. The major tasks simply would have been informing the miners of product availability and price, and making the product accessible to them.

Using this story as a background, let us extend it hypothetically. Presume that Levi Strauss had decided to establish a new division to manufacture and distribute blue jeans in Denver, Colorado during the Colorado gold and silver mining rush of the 1890s and early 1900s. Presume further that the new division was the only manufac-

turer of blue jeans in the territory for a number of years and was able
to meet the constantly growing demand until the population in the
area had grown sufficiently to attract another manufacturer who recognized there was room in the market for another supplier. Now ask,
what business orientation would have been appropriate for the second manufacturer who entered the same market later?

Would it not be reasonable to take the position that, as long as
demand is still growing fast, all the second supplier would have to
do is produce basically the identical product, but succeed by devising better promotion, distribution, and possibly lower pricing?
That is the gist of a sales orientation. If the new supplier were
more skilled in marketing and invested more heavily in these aspects of the marketing mix, it is conceivable that it could be a successful strategy.

Let us extend the hypothetical example to include the entrance of
an enterprising third supplier to the Denver area. Presume that, by the
time the third supplier has arrived on the scene, a significant number
of cowboys had moved into the area, herding cattle to the Denver
market; and a similar growth had taken place in farming in the surrounding plains to provide food to the growing Denver population.

On arriving to the Denver area, the third supplier surveys the situation and realizes that the Denver market for blue jeans is not just
one market, but several markets, each having different product (and
other marketing mix) requirements. For instance, there are miners
who wear out their jeans mainly on the knees while working in the
mines over in the hills; there are cowboys who wear out their jeans
on the seat and thighs and come into the outskirts of town to deliver
cattle; and there are farmers who want durable work clothing made
of blue denim, but don't want pants alone. They want bib overalls
instead, because overalls protect the entire body and provide better
ventilation during hot summer months. They live on the plains outside Denver, but also come into town to deliver produce.

The hallmark of market orientation is the mental discipline to always view any broadly described "market" as one which is composed of definable, narrower market segments, each with different
requirements, justifying different products and other marketing
variations, including different prices.

The groundwork is now in place to illustrate why the market orientation can produce above-average profits. The third blue jeans supplier to the Denver area realizes that, if jeans were designed and manufactured for miners with extra patches on the knees, the pants would last twice as long. If jeans for cowboys were designed and manufactured with extra material on the seats and thighs, these jeans would also last twice as long. Both miners and cowboys realize that jeans that last twice as long would be worth a lot more—almost twice as much; or at least, say, fifty percent more. Presume that the cost of manufacturing jeans with extra patches in the right places is only about ten percent more for miners and twenty percent more for cowboys than the original product cost, and that the demand is such for each that economies of scale in manufacture will not suffer when the more specialized production is initiated.

When all these conditions are met, the situation exists where the significantly higher value of the unmet customer need (for longer-lasting jeans) is captured with a significantly higher-priced product that does not cost proportionately more to make and market. Thus, a higher profit can result, and continue as long as the differential advantage can be sustained.

This example is clearly oversimplified, especially regarding competitive structure, to illustrate certain points. No recognition is given to the possible emotive value of having the newest style of jeans with patches in the correct places. The price of the product would be limited ultimately by the price and value of other generic substitute pants available. Yet, the amazing message from this hypothetical example is that the same principle applies in markets for any product, whether for aerospace/defense, machine tools, athletic equipment, chemicals and plastic components for automobiles and appliances, or any other product. Higher profits result from correctly priced differentiated products designed to meet user needs of significant value in specific product markets. The higher profits might be sustained for some period of time by achieving competitive advantages from several possible sources, such as patents, brand image, higher quality, established market position, and so forth.

The net result is that a market-oriented view will contribute directly to continual success in new product innovation. The whole organization becomes attuned to identifying unmet needs with higher value in target market segments where higher profits can be realized.

Functional Product-Market Definition

It has been interesting to observe over the years that among executives of firms that have not yet become market-oriented, the response upon hearing such an example (as the blue jeans) is almost always the same. It is something like, "Yeah, I can see how it could work in that business, but *ours* is different." They will usually go on to explain that they don't have the opportunity to differentiate their product to meet the needs of particular market segments the way our example showed. Yet, in every instance, the concept was eventually applied with success to all these businesses.

With the assistance of Dr. E. Jerome McCarthy, we devised the four-part definitional model called *product market*, shown in Figure 12, to aid management teams in becoming market-oriented. We then coached management team members in defining their existing businesses using this model, by identifying individual product-market segments, which previously had been treated as a whole. In using this definitional model with many firms, we made a significant discovery. As long as a firm defines and manages its businesses in terms of functional product-markets, as defined in the figure, it remains market ori-

---

Product-Market Definition

- *What*
    1. Product type

- *To meet what*
    2. Customer (user) functional need

- *For what*
    3. Type of customer

- *Where*
    4. Geographic area served

Figure 12

ented. The concept has a built-in reinforcement effect to prevent backsliding into a comfortable sales or production orientation.

Definition of *Product*

The definitional model outlined in Figure 12 uses the concept of product to include everything a firm provides to satisfy needs of customers in a selected product-market segment. Thus, the concept includes both physical and nonphysical properties of the product, and includes services as a form of nonphysical product. When properly conceived, each aspect of the product would satisfy customer needs and thereby have some value to the customer. The definition brings immediate attention to everything that is done for a given customer, such as providing a physical product with certain packaging and/or the nonphysical product, such as technical support and training. The definitional process also brings focus to the value of each customer functional need met by the product in each product-market segment.

Very often, the result of this focus is the realization that certain nonphysical aspects of the product, such as technical support service, obviously have high value to certain customers, but the value has not been captured in the pricing of the product. The resulting definitions also frequently reveal costly product features that historically have been included for all product-markets, yet have little or no value to some customers. For example, special molding equipment and plastic materials to facilitate quick changes in colors for exact color matching might be provided as part of a standard product which is not needed in some applications.

Definition of *Functional Need*

The second part of the definitional model is the description of the functions that are served (needs that are met) by the total product offering. In short, what does the product do for the customer in the product-market segment? We originally used a three-part definition of product-markets, limited to (1) a product for a (2) customer in a (3) geographical area. We added the fourth, functional, component to the definition after working with many technically trained managers in the aerospace and chemical industries whose education and careers had led them to a preoccupation with the features of the product to the exclusion of what value the functions served by those features had to customers.

We found that managers in technology-oriented (driven) companies (another form of production orientation) typically view their markets in terms of the products they make, rather than the functions performed by the product for the customers who buy and/or use the product. For example, if you ask an aerospace executive what markets the firm is in, you'd probably hear a list of products; gyros, flight data computers, airborne radar, and so forth. Or, if you ask an executive of a chemical company manufacturing plastics, you'd get a list such as polyethylene film, ABS, and polycarbonate. This view is not completely illogical, since the nature of the product does imply the functions to some extent, especially if you are technically trained and know that ABS plastics are not used for exactly the same products (functions) as polycarbonates.

When the functional component is added to the definition, it clarifies not only why each product-market requires differences in products, but also signals the differences in value of the product resulting from the differences in functions required. The extra step in defining the functions focuses managerial thought processes toward meeting customer needs and capturing value.

Definition of *Customer*

Often, executives of firms manufacturing component materials and parts view their customer simply as "who we sell to," rather than the end user of the final total product or system of which their component is a part. We found this view to be widespread among firms serving industrial/commercial and aerospace/defense markets. In all these cases, a firm's product is seldom the total finished product sold directly to the end user. For example, a flight management computer for military and commercial aircraft is part of a larger flight management system, or an integrated flight control system is part of the total aircraft.

Even when a final product is manufactured, it is usually sold, financed, distributed, and serviced through intermediaries of various types. All the intermediaries also have needs that have value that can be met by proper design of the product's physical and nonphysical properties. The properties include packaging, sales literature, technical literature, design consultation, and so forth.

All these considerations have led to our defining the customer to include the final user plus the middleman back to the manufacturer. This procedure highlights the fact that throughout the channels functional needs exist which have value and should be considered in designing the total product.

Definition of *Geography*

The fourth component in the product-market definition is the geographical area where the customer is to be served. The inclusion of the geographical dimension leads to a later consideration of whether one or several marketing strategies will be needed to address all areas. For example, if the end users of the same silicone sealant for construction of commercial office buildings are located worldwide, different marketing strategies involving different marketing mixes will be needed on different continents and often in different countries.

Marketing Strategy, Mix, and Plan

The reason a firm remains market oriented as long as it uses the four-part product-market definition to manage its businesses is that each product-market has its own marketing strategy and associated marketing plan. Management is constantly asked what are we, or should we be, doing for those customers in *that* product-market? This centers the focus on the unmet needs and their value to those specific customers. We can then concentrate on what product and other elements of the marketing strategy are required to meet those needs. Definitions of the terms marketing strategy and marketing mix are shown in Figure 13.[9]

A marketing strategy consists of a definition of a target product-market together with the specification of a marketing mix to serve

---

**A Marketing Strategy for A
Given Product-Market**

Includes

1. Definition of the target market (including basis
   for segmentation)

2. Specification of the 4 P's:
   - Product ⎫
   - Place ⎬ The Marketing Mix
   - Promotion ⎬
   - Price ⎭

All of which require detailed understanding of
customer need.

Figure 13

that product-market. A marketing mix consists of the four P's: total
product plus the promotion, pricing, and place (method of distribution) needed to meet certain needs in the target product-market.

Note at the bottom of the figure that there are needs in every aspect of the marketing mix, not only the product, that must be identified and, if properly met, offer the potential to capture value. Typical
needs (and sources of value) associated with the place, promotion,
and pricing in the marketing mix are shown in Figure 14.

A marketing plan is logically the fleshing out of functional details of the marketing strategy to include the anticipated revenues,
costs, and profits, together with financial controls needed, as shown
in Figure 15.[10]

Thus, the new product innovation process can be viewed as flow-
ing logically from the definition of needs and value in defined target

---

**Other Elements of The Marketing
Mix Also Satisfy Needs**

1. The place(s) where and when product is available for purchase

2. The promotion-information provided, image created

3. The price(s), with and without options, credit availability and terms

---

Figure 14

A Product-Market Plan
Is A Product-Market Strategy Plus

Time-related details for implementing the strategy

- Target market ⎱
- Marketing mix ⎰ The product-market strategy
- Resources–at what rate
- Expected–sales
- Expected–profits
- Control

The product-market plan

Figure 15

product-markets to the specification of requirements for all elements of the marketing mix to determination of the expected financial results of the entire action, and then to plans for execution and control of the strategy.

Examples of Functional Product-Market Definitions for Blue Jeans

In the hypothetical blue jeans case, when the first (production-oriented) manufacturer began operation in Denver, a three-part definition of the broad product-market would have been adequate. It might have been defined as follows:

Blue jeans for males in the Denver area

Product: Durable pants made from blue denim
Customer: Male residents and transients
Geography: Denver and surrounding territory

The entire market was thus seen as one product-market with one marketing mix for all customers.

This same view of the product-market would have sufficed for the second (sales-oriented) supplier. The product would have been the same for both suppliers, but the second supplier probably introduced changes in promotion, pricing, and place (methods of distribution) in order to gain entry into the same product-market.

The third supplier (who was market-oriented) recognized that the one broad product-market could be viewed as (at least) three narrower product-markets with different functional product needs, and possibly different needs in the marketing mix as well. These three product-markets might have been named as follows:

Blue jeans pants to withstand heavy wear in knees for miners in mountains west of Denver

Product: Durable blue denim pants with reinforced knees
Function: All-purpose wear, but withstanding heavy abrasive wear in knees
Customers: Miners
Geography: Mountainous territories within 100 miles west of Denver

Blue jeans pants to withstand heavy wear in thighs and seats for cowboys in plains around Denver

Product: Durable blue denim pants with reinforced seats and inner thighs
Function: All-purpose wear, but withstanding heavy abrasive wear in seats and inner thighs
Customers: Cowboys and ranchers
Geography: Plains within 100 miles east, south, and north of Denver

Blue jeans bib overalls to withstand heavy wear for farmers around Denver

Product: Durable overalls made of blue denim
Function(s): All-purpose wear, but protecting entire torso and legs, and providing ventilation for cooling in hot weather
Customers: Farmers and farm hands
Geography: Farms within 100 miles of Denver

Note that none of the definitions include nonphysical properties in this simplified example. Also note that each title reflects the three or four parts of each definition. The single broad product-market title mentioned only product, customer, and geography, whereas the narrow product-market definitions also include a brief description of function as well.

If the market-oriented supplier of blue jeans were to initially consider these three narrow product-markets as a potentially suitable
basis for addressing the total market, it would be necessary to determine all requirements, not just those for product alone. The necessary requirements research thus would have to encompass all
elements of the marketing mix for each product-market. Fortunately, while analyzing the different product requirements in each
product-market, it takes very little additional effort to understand
the remaining requirements.

Assuming that the three narrow product-markets provide a basis
for success, each product-market would normally have its own marketing strategy and associated product-market plan for implementation and control. Thus, the sustained marketing orientation would
have led to focusing on unmet needs, determining the value (to the
customer) of those needs, then determining how new products
might be developed and translated into successful product-market
strategies and plans. This scenario illustrates why a market orientation naturally leads toward success in new product innovation.

But there is much more needed to ensure success. The first
questions are whether the firm should be in the clothing business
in the first place and, if so, in blue jeans, and why in Denver?
These questions point to the overriding importance of setting direction and determining opportunity selection criteria to guide
new product selection.

Changing to a Market Orientation

It is usually not easy for a management team to change its thinking
from a production or sales orientation to a marketing orientation. It
may require several years to complete the transition. To accomplish
this transition, we often begin by redefining the business as a group
of broad product-markets, using the three-part definition—product,
customers, and geography, as illustrated in the blue jeans example.

After operating the business with broad product-market strategies
and plans for a year or two, the management team begins to identify
major narrow product markets using the four-part definition—product, function, customer, and geography—and develops individual

strategies and plans for each product-market. The business may be managed as a combination of broad and narrow product markets for another year or so until all product-markets have been defined and appropriate strategies and plans developed. An example of such a progression in product-market definitions for a portion of an aerospace division of Lear Siegler, Inc., (now Smith Industries) is shown in Figure 16.

After completing the transition, the management team at Lear Siegler, Inc., reported that they increased the sales and profits of the operation following each stage in the progression. The total transition required two years to assimilate.

**Evolution from Product Line
to
Narrow Product-Market Definitions**

Product Line

• Flight Management Systems

Broad Product-Markets

• Flight Management Systems for Commercial Aircraft Worldwide

• Flight Management Systems for Military Aircraft Worldwide

• Funded Advanced Development (R & D) of Flight Management Systems for Military Aircraft in the United States

Narrow Product-Markets

• Performance Data Computer for Flight Management of Boeing 767s Sold to Airlines Worldwide

• Performance Data Computer for Flight Management of Boeing 767s Sold to Boeing Aircraft Co. in Seattle, Washington

---

Figure 16

7

The Value of
Opportunity Selection Criteria

On countless occasions, when management teams have just
learned about Planned Innovation, they acknowledge that
their firm needs help in learning how to determine new product requirements, but they don't need selection criteria, either because
"Everyone already knows what kind of products we need" or "We
tried using such criteria, but they weren't of much help."

Whenever we hear such comments, we know that firm is about to
get a big, pleasant surprise because, formulated with the correct inputs from the right people, opportunity selection criteria can be
enormously valuable to any firm. Yet, among firms which use some
form of criteria, the potential power is often not realized because the
criteria do not have the correct inputs from the right people and/or
the criteria are used ineffectively.

Because of the widespread misunderstanding regarding the potential power of correctly formulated opportunity selection criteria,
no area in the Planned Innovation process has received greater attention. We have experimented and tested formats and procedures
with hundreds of management teams at various corporate levels
from the top down. From this intense involvement, we have concluded that opportunity selection criteria should contain four major
components, as shown in Figure 17.

Opportunity Selection Criteria

Assures selection of existing and new opportunities that:

1 **Meet business mission, goals and objectives**
   • Qualitatively: By defining preferred kind of product-markets
   • Quantitatively: By indicating desired amount of sales and profitability

2 **Match resources to opportunities**
   • Qualitatively: By indicating key capabilities (strengths) to be used
   • Quantitatively: By defining minimum and maximum levels of sales,
                       R & D, investment and profitability desired

3 **Have a strong basis for competitive advantage and competitive opening**

4 **Are reinforced by favorable long-run external trends without bucking any**

Figure 17

First, the criteria should provide guidance as to how the business mission, goals, and objectives might be accomplished by qualitatively defining the kind of product-markets the firm desires to enter, or continue to serve, as well as those the firm does not wish to enter, or continue serving. Quantitative guidance is needed as well. This can be effectively communicated by specifying the total sales growth and profits needed to reach the firm's financial goals and functional objectives, indicating what portion of that growth is needed from new or modified products each year over the planning horizon.

Second, the criteria should indicate, qualitatively and quantitatively, what kinds and amounts of resources would most likely produce the best matching of existing and potentially available resources to new product market opportunities. This requires identification and communication of the key capabilities, or strengths, that management feels should be used. We always suggest leading from strength, as in playing no trump in contract bridge. Criteria should also express how small or large any new opportunity should be, in terms of a profile of sales growth, and critical amounts of resources needed in R & D, manufacturing, and marketing, so that the new product can be resourced comfortably by the firm and achieve suitable profitability. Often, separate quantitative criteria need to be devised for modification and extensions of existing products.

Third, opportunity selection criteria should indicate the most probable bases of future competitive advantage in preferred product-markets. Such advantages can stem from technical strengths in R & D and manufacturing, but can also occur from market position and strength in distribution. Criteria for competitive openings are often derived from historically successful patterns, such as a reputation for being first with new technology, to the opposite extreme of always being a follower, or waiting for the competition to stumble.

Fourth, selection criteria should indicate any recognized external trends which are likely to affect new product opportunities in preferred future product-markets. Again, these trends are often technical in nature, but may relate to economic, social, demographic, or political forces shaping markets, and on a global basis.

Selection Versus Screening Criteria

In our first and second editions of *Planned Innovation,* we used the term *product-market screening criteria* instead of opportunity selection criteria. The introduction of this new term is not solely a change in semantics. It represents a significant difference in philosophical emphasis, which we have discovered to have enormous power.

The important difference between selection and screening lies in the difference between a proactive and a reactive use of such criteria. Our initial emphasis was on properly sorting out opportunities from among a number of new or existing product-market opportunities, principally to assure a good fit with the firm's resources and objectives. Our new emphasis is on developing a sense of selective perception to guide the initial thought processes of everyone within a firm. The net result is essentially the same type of criteria, but developed with greater emphasis on proper managerial input to reflect the strategic and tactical objectives and strengths of various business units within a firm. This approach usually calls for a top management team to develop a broad umbrella set of criteria for the firm, followed by the framing of more specific criteria by divisional or business unit management teams. The approach also requires broad communication and explanation of the criteria throughout the business units to stimulate the recognition of the type of new opportunities desired.

When such a concept of selective perception is implemented, good new opportunities seem to appear from everywhere.

Most of us almost unconsciously experience the unusual power of selective perception every day in our lives. Every time you buy a new dress or sports jacket, you immediately notice if someone else happens to wear the same article. When we first purchase a new or different car, we suddenly begin to see all the cars just like it, which we never noticed before. Sometimes, in a room full of people, we hear the voice of a loved one standing out among many voices because, over the years, our ears have developed a selective filter for that voice. Advertisers spend millions to develop selective perception, so that shoppers in a supermarket will see their product stand out against a background of similar products on the shelf.

A similar selective perception for new product opportunities can be developed within a firm. When it is achieved, the result and feeling are much like the following example experienced by one of the authors. While he was away at college, his parents moved to a small town on a slender peninsula of land in Virginia called the "Northern Neck," bounded by the Rappahannock River on the west and the Potomac on the east. Every visit home during semester breaks included a field trip to the nearby beaches along the Potomac, where his parents loved to look for fossilized sharks' teeth which washed out of the adjacent marl cliffs during storms. At first, it was difficult for him to find any specimens unless they were totally exposed on the beach. His parents, however, could find them by detecting slightly irregular "bumps" in the smooth sand. When he asked them how they could be so perceptive, they answered, almost in unison, "You just have to know what you are looking for." Later, when he learned exactly what he was looking for, he, too, became expert in finding them. (The largest specimen found by this trio, measuring some eight inches from tip to base, was proudly presented by his parents to the Smithsonian for display.)

This form of selective perception can be taught to everyone in an organization, so that all are constantly on the lookout for the right kind of new opportunities because they, too, know what to look for. In this important way, management can provide guidance to the new product innovation activities, starting at the very beginning with idea conception.

Despite the initial concern often voiced by scientists and engineers that such selection criteria may inhibit the creative process, just the opposite has proven to be true. Such criteria actually stimulate the creative process by providing assurance that any new product which meets the parameters will likely lead to success (without exactly specifying the details of the product).

Selection Criteria Can Also Be Used for Screening

An important bonus from our new emphasis on selection versus screening of new products is that you can "have your cake and eat it, too." The same criteria can be used to sort out or prioritize existing or new business opportunities. In the process of developing selection criteria, we suggest that criteria be tested by determining whether they would have sorted out successful from unsuccessful past or current businesses. As a practical matter, when selection criteria are first being established within a business, the initial task is usually to establish priorities among existing research projects or existing product-markets.

Neither selection nor screening can be meaningfully accomplished, however, unless the criteria have been developed with proper managerial input. This means that the criteria must reflect a true consensus, based on thoughtfully conceived objectives and honest assessment of strengths and weaknesses. In our experience, it is not a task to be delegated to a single person, not even the CEO. No one person can do the strategic and tactical planning nor have sufficient depth of understanding of all strengths and weaknesses. Furthermore, effective understanding and support for such criteria requires a consensus-building, rather than a "dictatorial," process.

Issues Involved in Opportunity Selection Process

Opportunity selection decisions can range from choices of modifications to existing products to identification of entirely new products for new markets. The problem also can be one of choosing among possible opportunities already identified, or one of finding new opportunities of the right kind in the first place.

Regardless of the specific character of the decision, there are always two major questions or issues to be resolved, each with associated sub-issues:

1. What do we (the firm) need
   a. strategically?
   b. tactically?
2. What *can* we (the firm) do
   a. with our capabilities and resources?
   b. given our strengths and weaknesses relative to competition?
   c. considering external factors, conditions, and trends to be expected in the business environment (over which we have little or no control)?

The analogy between employing a sophisticated passing offense in football and a well-managed new product innovation program is useful in illustrating these two major issues and their sub-issues. First, in choosing which plays (opportunities) to call, the quarterback (or business team leader) must consider: (a) Strategically, what field position does the team (firm) need at this point in the game, and (b) Tactically, what play (opportunity) or sequence of plays would advance the team (firm) to that position?

Second, the quarterback must consider: (a) Which plays (opportunities) can the team execute given the talent, speed, size, and physical strength of the players? Next, consideration must be given to: (b) Which of the plays (new product opportunities) could be executed successfully, given the strengths of the opposing team (competition) relative to our team (firm)?

The coach or quarterback must consider how the execution of various plays (opportunities) will likely be influenced (positively or negatively) by external conditions, such as intensity and direction of wind, presence of rain or snow, turf conditions, and the psychological influence of home team advantage. In business, external conditions can be categorized as technical, demographic, political, economic, and social factors.

Given the number of considerations that must be taken into account as plays are called in the heat of a game, it is understandable that decision making is often shared between the coach (with help from his staff) and the quarterback on the field. The same is true in business, where the coach is analogously top management and the quarterback is the manager of operations. It makes sense that the coach on the sideline will have a better view of the strategic issues, as does top management in business. Furthermore, as it makes sense in football at critical points in a game to call time-out so that the quarterback can come to the sideline to consult and share his views with the coach, it also makes good sense in business that the strategic and tactical issues are addressed in a consultative manner from time to time between levels of management. In businesses, the operational effectiveness of management of new product innovation is greatly enhanced when different levels of management among multifunctional departments participate in the development of a (written) statement of opportunity selection criteria.

Importance of Integrating Strategy and Tactics

Although the forward pass in football provides a dynamic offense, as does new product innovation in business, the analogy suggests that play selection is a process of choosing among well-known, practiced alternatives. Seldom is this the case with new product innovation in business. Even with modifications and extensions of existing products, creative solutions are required and new unknowns must be addressed almost every time.

Thus, in developing opportunity selection criteria, it is more useful to take a proactive posture and address the question, "What type of opportunities are we seeking?" This immediately raises the same issues, but in a new light. This view focuses attention on what the firm is trying to accomplish strategically, as a total business, and how each business unit can contribute tactically to the overall purpose, to the point of identifying how each product-market plan within each business unit fits into the total scheme of things. Even the tactical decisions associated with the development and implementation of marketing mixes (including new product activities) for each product-market must then synergistically support the strategic thrust of the business.

The integration of tactical actions with strategic objectives provides a bridge between the two major concerns which must be resolved in opportunity selection: "What the firm needs" and "What the firm can do." Both must be addressed in every case; it makes no sense to create grandiose strategic plans if there is no chance the firm can execute them nor to devise tactical product-market plans that can be successful in themselves, but don't contribute to the overall thrust of the business.

Matching Resources to Opportunities

In order to address what the firm can do with its capabilities and resources, without competitive considerations, and what the firm can do, considering its strengths and weaknesses relative to competition, we introduced the concept of matching resources to opportunities. The concept says that a firm can complete the new product development, manufacture, and marketing if it has (or can obtain) the capabilities and resources to meet all requirements. Moreover, a firm can succeed with any new product innovation, provided that the capabilities and resources provide adequate strength relative to competing firms in the specified product markets.

External factors beyond the control of the firm, such as long-run economic, technical, and demographic trends, also must be identified and used to modify the requirements needed for success. For example, if the trend in the design and production of special computer chips is toward more powerful personal computers with free software installed, the requirements for reliability, software support, and (no) maintenance must be reflected in the statement of total product-market requirements.

Success Must Be Tactical and Strategic

The two major errors we have observed in the mismatch of resources to opportunity are highlighted in Figure 18.

Matching Resources to Opportunities

- *Identify* strengths and weaknesses, then,

- *Lead* from strengths

- *Avoid*

  - Spreading resources too thin on opportunities that are too large or too complex (technically or managerially)

  - Pursuing opportunities that are too small or too simple (technically or managerially)

(The matching of resources must be done both quantitatively and qualitatively.)

Figure 18

A tactical failure is a failure in the physical or nonphysical product to meet the unmet need, or a failure in some other aspect of the marketing strategy and plan, whether in promotion, pricing, or place (distribution). It often results from a mismatch of resources to opportunity, or a miscalculation of the competitive opening or advantage. The spreading of resources too thinly on too many opportunities, or on opportunities that are too large is widely recognized. Tactical mistakes also can be made at the other end of the spectrum, by pursuing opportunities that are too small or too simple, and that could be more economically addressed by smaller competitors. Tactical failure usually occurs within a relatively short time after introduction of the product. It could be in weeks or months, depending of the length of the underlying product-market life cycle.

A strategic failure is the type where the firm develops and markets a product that does not really contribute synergistically to its longer-run objectives. The product often is a tactical success, which compounds the strategic failure by encouraging the firm to devote more and more resources to it, leading further into a blind canyon. The firm may recoup part or all of its investment by divesting the product, but it never recovers the loss from the opportunity cost of time and effort spent in a direction that does not fully pay off.

This was unfortunately the case with the development of the Mailmobile® system by the former Lear Siegler, Inc., (now Smith Industries) in an attempt to diversify from the aerospace industry. The Mailmobile® was developed for delivery of mail, documents, and supplies in large office buildings housing banks, insurance companies, corporate headquarters, and so forth. The Mailmobile® was a spectacular tactical success, but its lack of strategic marketing fit with the resources available to the aerospace firm ultimately led to its divesture to Bell and Howell, a major firm in the office equipment field.

We have found that management teams, perhaps logically, tend to place too much focus on achieving tactical success in new product innovation, often to the detriment of strategic success. This is why, in later years, we have placed greater emphasis on multilevel managerial team involvement in developing opportunity selection criteria. The payoff occurs when multiple tactical successes synergistically combine to product an exceptional strategic success.

Lear Siegler, Inc., did achieve combined tactical and strategic successes with Data Transfer Modules and Solid-State Flight Data Recorders developed for military aircraft. These products produced dramatic sales growth with excellent profits as well.

The Data Transfer Module was originally developed for transfer of mission data to the F-4 fighter plane. Additional models were then developed for other aircraft. A similar pattern was followed with the Solid-State Flight Data Recorder. It was originally developed for the F-16 to help resolve why unexplained incidents were occurring. The product was extended through other designs to ultimately include twenty-eight different types of military aircraft. In both cases, each new (modified) product was a tactical success which, over the years, resulted in solid strategic success as well.

This was also the case for the Donnelly Corporation when a series of tactical successes with new glass products for the auto industry, mentioned in Chapter 1, led to the growth pattern shown there.

Experiences such as those cited above at Lear Siegler, Inc., and the Donnelly Corporation led to the realization that a complete

---

Charateristics of a Desirable Opportunity

- The existence of an unmet customer need of significant value to a present or potential customer, which

- A firm (division) can solve, and make a suitable profit doing so, and

- Advance the business toward both its tactical and strategic goals and objectives.

Figure 19

success with new product innovation should be defined as one that includes the combination of both tactical and strategic success. This realization is reflected in the suggested definition in Figure 19 of what should constitute a desirable new product opportunity for a market-oriented firm.

8

Obtaining Proper Inputs to Opportunity Selection Criteria

The key requirement for framing effective opportunity selection criteria is that proper inputs are received from the proper people. Inputs are needed concerning each of the four sections of the selection criteria, including: (1) business mission, goals, and objectives; (2) matching resources to opportunities; (3) basis for competitive opening and advantage; and (4) external long-range trends.

In working with many businesses and management teams over the years, we have come to the conclusion that the essential elements in providing effective strategic guidance are achieving thoughtful, multifunctional management consensus; recording that consensus in written form; and communicating this consensus to the lower levels of operational management, encouraging discussion and critique from those with more detailed knowledge of specific capabilities of people, equipment, and relative strengths of competitors.

Effective guidance can be obtained by developing three written documents based on consensus-building discussions among members of the management team. These include specially designed statements of mission, financial goals, and functional objectives. Mission statements alone do not provide an adequate basis for communicating to others within the organization. It is the combination of the three interlocking statements, presenting information in qualitative and quantitative form, that provides the necessary basis for discussion, critique, and, ultimately, the communication of understanding.

Mission Statements Guide New Product Innovation

Mission statements generally are written to impress others *outside* the business, such as customers, individual and institutional investors, governmental regulatory agencies, and so forth. It seems they are rarely written expressly to provide guidance for others *inside* the firm.

By observing the kind of strategic input needed by lower-level functional managers so that they can give proper direction to new product innovation activities, we devised the five-point outline shown in Figure 20.

The most basic input needed by mid- and lower-level managers is "Where does top management see our firm now?" Then, given that benchmark, they need to know what top management's vision of the future is, and what the scope of product-markets to be served is. This includes whether the firm may exit any present markets. Next, and always critical to engineering and manufacturing managers, is which technologies will continue to be used, which developed or acquired, and which will be discarded or not acquired. Finally, all

---

Outline of Mission Statement

1. Where are we *now*? Or, what is the situation now?

2. What is the *thrust* of the business or our vision of the future?

3. What is the scope of product-markets to be served now and in the future?

4. What is the scope of technology to be used in products and processes, and what is the technology that will *not* be used, if any?

5. What is the relative emphasis to be placed on sales growth versus profits?

Figure 20

functional managers need guidance concerning the relative emphasis to be placed on growing the business (sales) versus improving or
maintaining profitability, as measured by ROI or earnings per share
of common stock, and so forth.

In constructing such mission statements, it is desirable and possible to condense the information to one typewritten page to be used
as an outline for open discussion among several levels of managers
in various functions to clarify the strategic direction of the business.

Statement of Financial Goals Needed

Lower levels of management also need a quantitative statement of
anticipated goals in terms of desired sales, profitability, and investments over the firm's planning horizon. This should include overall
sales and profitability expected year by year, as well as any estimated gap in sales anticipated, based on the difference between anticipated future sales from existing product-market plans and the
overall future sales objective. An estimate should then be made as to
how the gap will be filled, based on sales of existing products to new
markets; modified or new products; and from acquisitions, licenses,
and joint ventures.

By stating the year when various amounts of sales must be generated from different degrees of product innovation (in order to
achieve sales and profit objectives), top management can send clear
direction to the organization regarding what it believes needs to be
done. And, by including the assumed investment amounts needed,
management is also saying to others in the firm, "We think this sales
and profit can be accomplished with this investment. What do you
think? Can it be done?"

Such a clarification of financial goals represents a more detailed
quantitative statement of what is meant by the mission statement.
The financial goals and the mission statement are thus interrelated,
and it is the combination of the two that provides total guidance.
Separate statements are often preferred, so that the mission statement can be circulated widely within the firm, while the statement
of financial goals is considered more proprietary, with circulation
limited to key management personnel.

The Role of Functional Objectives

Because the financial gap analysis raises many questions regarding feasibility of implementation, it does not achieve final value in providing guidance until the functional departments have examined the consequences, determined the critical issues regarding implementation, and possibly recommended changes in the numbers. This critical examination can be accomplished by having the functional managers identify what must be done in each function, and when, to achieve the financial goals within the context of the mission statement.

After completing this task, the review of the functional objectives by the whole management team usually discloses several critical issues which must be given special attention. By defining the mission statement, financial goals, functional objectives, and critical issues, a multifunctional management team accomplishes a great deal toward defining a logical business development program, including new product innovation, that will move the company toward its objectives as defined in both qualitative and quantitative terms. In so doing, the team establishes the general magnitude and type of activity needed, especially in determining if new products, modified products, and/or acquisitions and joint ventures will be needed.

Defining Capabilities, Strengths, and Weaknesses

The second major question, "What can we (the firm) do?" is also addressed within the conceptual framework of matching resources to opportunities. To implement the concept, management must realistically define the firm's capabilities, strengths, and weaknesses, and recognize bases for competitive openings and advantage.

In terms of our football example, a capability is a forward pass play our team (firm) can (knows how to) execute, whereas a strength is the ability to execute the play successfully against a known competitor in a given game (product-market). Of course, the outcome is also affected by external factors. In business, a firm can define its individual capabilities (plays) without reference to competition, but a firm cannot define its strengths in absolute terms.

A firm's strength must be defined relative to competition in a given product-market. Furthermore, we conceptualize that a firm's strength is made up of a unique combination of underlying general capabilities, which are likewise composed of more specific capabilities. The three-tier definitional concept is shown in Figure 21.

We have found it useful to characterize a firm's strength as a large rope, such as used on a barge or ocean liner. The rope (strength) is made of large strands we initially defined as general capabilities, and the large strands are composed of smaller threads, which we term specific capabilities.

The crisscrossing arrows in Figure 21 connecting the three tiers of definition have special significance. They illustrate the additional concept that different combinations of specific capabilities can make up different general capabilities and, likewise, different combinations of general capabilities can define different strengths.

In the process of definition, we have found that the greater the detail in which a capability is defined, the more easily it can be defined

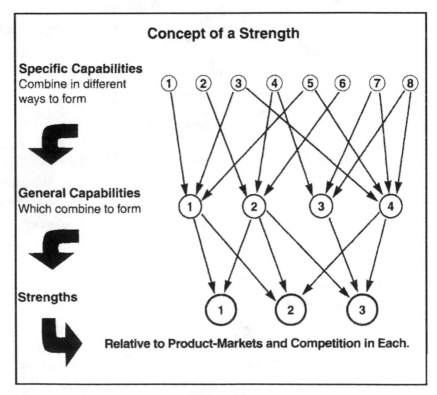

Figure 21

without reference to competition in specified product-markets. For example, the specific capability to blend plastic resins to maintain exact color matching from batch to batch in manufacturing housing for appliances, power tools, and toys can be defined without reference to competition. Whether or not this capability can contribute to a strength depends on the importance of exactness in color matching in a given product-market, and the abilities of the competition. Exact color matching may be very important in some kitchen appliances, less important in small children's toys, and not important at all in housings for large power tools.

Obviously, a large firm may have many capabilities. To achieve practicality in applying the three-tier definitional concept, a logical procedure is needed to provide focus. Our procedure is to have the management team define the firm's (or division's) *present* two or three major broad product-markets using the four-part definitional concept (product, function, customer, and geography).

We next have them identify the strongest two or three competitors for each product-market defined. These steps provide a focus for the top management team to define the two or three general capabilities they feel lead to the firm's strengths in these major product-markets. These are frequently in technical R & D, manufacturing techniques and capacities, and marketing and distribution, and, occasionally, in finance and general management. At this point in the definition process, we strive to limit the number of general capabilities being considered to a total of three to six.

We next bring in two or three next-level managers and technicians in each functional area to assist the management team in identifying the (three to six) *specific* capabilities which combine to form each *general* capability already defined by the top management team. This usually results in the definition of a total of twelve to fifteen specific capabilities. The number varies depending on the size of firm and number of divisions being considered.

The final step is to examine the list of general and specific capabilities in light of possible *future* product-markets of interest to the firm. The presence of particular capabilities may be interpreted as strengths relative to anticipated competition in present or future product-markets. A weakness is the opposite side of the same coin.

A present or potential weakness is the absence of specific or general capabilities needed for success relative to competition in a present or future product-market.

When we began using this definitional process with the Donnelly Corporation, a major manufacturer of automotive rear vision products, the management team identified general capabilities in marketing, research and development, engineering, finance, and production. One of the general capabilities identified in production was defined simply as "Good Glass Handling." When pressed for more specific detail, they initially responded that everyone in the firm knew what that meant. They were satisfied that similar levels of definition of general capabilities would be adequate for guiding new product activities.

An example of the firm's strengths in their major broad product-market, defined simply as Rear Vision Devices for automobile Original Equipment Manufacturers (OEMs), is shown in Figure 22.

This firm operated with reasonable success for a year or two after defining its capabilities at this general level without defining the more specific capabilities. Then, after an annual management review of its new product development activities, the next level of detail was added, which had a profound effect on the future growth of

---

Example of Combination of General Capabilities to Form A Strength

1. "Good glass handling capability,"
   plus

2. Proven reliable supplier to certain industry segments,
   plus

3. Certain specific research & engineering skills in specific technologies,
   plus

4. Certain size financial resource,
   plus

5. Specialized production know-how or equipment, etc.

Figure 22

Example of Specific Capabilities

"State-of-the-art production skills in cleaning, cutting, bending, and laminating medium to high volume quantities of standard float glass, standard sheet, and tempered glass in sizes of .5 to 5 square feet and thicknesses in the range of .1 to .5 inches."

These specific capabilities combine to form the general capability

"Good glass-handling capability"

Figure 23

the firm. Note the numerous specific capabilities which form the threads of definition for "Good Glass Handling" (general capability) shown in the Figure 23.

The richness provided by the added detail is instantly apparent. When taken together with the definition of other specific capabilities underlying the other general capabilities in various functional areas, a new perspective emerged. Members of the management team from different functions were able to reach consensus as to which combinations of capabilities would produce the greatest strengths in product-markets identified for future growth. The deepened understanding ultimately led to the successful development of a wide range of new products based on specific capabilities in glass handling together with other specific capabilities in research and development, production, finance, and marketing.

When management teams representing different functional departments have not participated in discussion of the firm's specific capabilities they often have difficulty reaching consensus about the firm's strengths. Without the depth of understanding provided by detailing specific capabilities, attempts to reach consensus often drift into an emotional debate among a group of strong personalities. We have seen the turf-protecting emotional exchanges between marketing and R & D executives, and between manufacturing and marketing managers, melt into harmony as soon as each one learns the specific capabilities (and deficiencies) of each other's departments.

Sound consensus building regarding strengths is even more difficult to achieve in large corporations where executives are mobile, being shifted to new positions every few years. In such cases, we have often found that only one or two members of a team may have much depth of understanding regarding the capabilities among different functional departments. The easy way out in such situations is for newer team members to defer to those with more depth of knowledge and experience. This often happens when the most experienced member of the team also has a strong personality. Consensus then really means "whatever Joe says is right." Of course, this can lead to tragic results if whatever Joe says is wrong!

We found this situation in a large aerospace division which had been recently acquired by the parent corporation. The parent corporation had appointed a new CEO from one of its other divisions, and the new CEO, in turn, had brought in a number of new managers with whom he had experience and whom he trusted. His assignment was to turn the failing division around. The new management team was composed largely of outsiders who did not know which of the insiders they should believe regarding the true strengths of the division.

The opening discussion was a round of turf-protecting statements with exaggerated claims—a perfect setup for impasse. However, by first defining the major product-markets being served and then shifting discussion to the general capabilities which provided strengths in those product-markets, the team was led into a detailed analysis of the specific capabilities underlying the general ones. The impasse was quickly broken. The greater level of detail provided an objective basis to view the division's true strengths in its major product-markets. An informed consensus was reached as to the major strengths the firm could use to attain new goals and objectives in product-markets that the team defined.

This does not mean that all specific capabilities need be considered in every new product innovation decision. Most new product activities actually involve modifications and extensions to present products for existing or moderately expanded markets. Once specific capabilities are internalized, frequently reccurring unique combinations are recognized as major general capabilities (also recently named "core competencies").[11] Most decisions can be made at the general capability level once the detail basis has been digested. In a similar manner, once the major or core general capabilities have been well understood, unique combinations of general capabilities become recognized as strengths relative to competition in familiar product-markets.

Management teams that have developed an in-depth understanding of the firm's specific and general capabilities through such a consensus-building process are prepared for better decision making for years ahead. With this background, strategic planning issues can be discussed intelligently in terms of well-recognized general capabilities, knowing how they combine to form strengths in present markets. When consideration is given to expansion to new markets with new products (for which general capabilities have not been well defined), the discussion can easily shift to the level of specific capabilities without emotional, turf-protecting debate. New general capabilities reflecting other possible unique combinations of specific capabilities can be defined and discussed within a logical framework.

Competitive Opening and Advantage

The opportunity selection process should always include identifying the reason for a competitive opening and the basis for competitive advantage, should the opportunity be pursued. Distinguishing between those two aspects of competition always clarifies what will be required for success with a new product innovation.

It is useful to define a competitive opening in terms of an event. What has happened to create the opening? Has a competitor's product failed to meet customer needs? Have the customer requirements changed because of related technological changes, such as new materials or processes? Has the government passed legislation that changes the requirements because of environmental or safety concerns? It might be that the external environment has drastically changed, such as the end of the Cold War, creating numerous new business opportunities in the Eastern bloc countries.

Whatever it is, an ideal opening is based on an identifiable event or series of events. But what if no such event can be identified? Could an opportunity exist nevertheless? Of course it could, but in that instance, an opening must be forged (or forced) as part of the marketing plan, with attendant higher costs than if the opening were based on an external event. This situation typically occurs when a firm achieves a technological advance that offers a much better, and often lower-cost, solution to an existing need or meets valuable unrecognized needs.

Both of these situations resulted when Toledo Scale, a major manufacturer of grocery scales, perfected the electronic load-cell technology that ultimately made its entire line of mechanical scales obsolete. The new electronic scales made it possible to weigh and calculate total price with such speed and precision that such scales are now commonplace in every supermarket and retail store.

The same technology made it possible to develop electronic digital scales that could be used for counting small, inexpensive parts where knowing the exact numbers was very valuable in receiving, manufacturing, shipping, and inventory of components. The unmet need for improved supermarket scales had been known for some time; creating the opening required little more than informing the customers of the availability. In the case of the new parts-counting scales, customers did not initially understand their own unmet need for such a product. The initial marketing mix had to include extra elements to inform, persuade, and instruct customers, all of which increased costs of product introduction.

Whether a competitive opening is realized because of an external event or is internally created by the firm, the opening alone is not sufficient for success. In fact, it can often be a trap. Ease of entry may prompt investment in a new opportunity, firms only learning later that there is no way to keep competition out long enough to achieve adequate returns. In short, competitive advantage is needed as well.

A competitive advantage is best characterized as "whatever keeps the competition out." A useful analogy is the Great Wall of China, built to keep out the Mongol hoards. But history shows that even the wall could not keep the adversary out forever. So it is in business. A competitive advantage is not going to last forever. It simply gives a firm a sustainable advantage for a sufficient length of time to reach its goals and objectives.

In many situations, especially in the electronic computer industry, the sufficient length of time can be very short—a few weeks or months. The executives of one such firm characterized this type of competitive advantage as "having no wall, but instead having faster ponies than the Mongols."

In business, there are many potential bases for competitive advantage, each with different lengths of time. Having a basic technical patent or, better, a group of patents, is well known to provide seventeen years of protection. But this depends on the strength of the patent(s), and whether alternative technical approaches to meeting the same needs can be found by competitors. Secret formulations, such as Coca-Cola, are often cited as the best ultimate protection from competitive inroads. It certainly has contributed to their long-term success, even though it didn't stop other colas from entering the market. It did provide sufficient protection for a long enough time for the firm to establish its brand recognition and market position, which are themselves bases for further advantage.

A firm rarely achieves its competitive advantage on one factor alone. It may get a foothold with one advantage, but it cannot rest on its oars. Additional protection can often be achieved through proprietary manufacturing processes or generally by doing a better job of meeting the customer's total need. Providing better packaging methods, technical assistance, or on-time delivery also contribute to sustaining an advantage. However, such examples can often be copied, eroding the competitive advantage within a short time.

Fortunately, when evaluating new product opportunities, it is usually possible to identify the probable bases for competitive advantage and the approximate length of time they will be effective. To proceed with product innovation without identifying the bases of protection from competitive inroads is an open invitation to disaster. We have found it is often much easier to enter a product-market (to seize an opening) with a new product than it is to stay in the market and achieve a suitable level of profitability in the face of an aroused, entrenched competitor. The positive identification of some basis of competitive advantage is an absolute requirement before proceeding with any new product innovation.

External Trends

In most football games, the external environmental conditions are usually easy to identify, although rapidly changing weather conditions may be difficult to predict on an hour-by-hour basis during a given contest. Nevertheless, external conditions usually can be expected to have a significant effect on the execution of certain plays and, therefore, can have a significant influence on the outcome of a game. During our years at Michigan, it always seemed that the last game of the season, traditionally played against Ohio State, was never played in good weather. We usually had to endure a snowstorm for at least part of the game. The combination of numbed fingers and slick footing reduced the effectiveness of the passing game, and often resulted in constant use of our "three yards and a cloud of dust (snow)" offense.

This type of thing can happen to businesses, also, with the same devastating results. And, often, it is generally predictable if given proper recognition during the opportunity selection and assessment process. After capabilities have been defined, we ask the same functional managers to also identify the (three to four) major external factors or long-run trends that are affecting the performance (both positively and negatively) of the function as it contributes to the firm's overall operation in each of the major present and anticipated future product-markets. For example, we have the manager of R & D identify the major long-run trends in technology, materials, and design methods. We have the manufacturing manager identify long-run trends in manufacturing methods, total quality assurance, and just-in-time delivery. We have the marketing manager identify the external trends affecting the value of the products and their anticipated life cycles in the major product-markets. To aid in the identification of external factors and trends, we have found a checklist of five broad categories to be helpful, as shown in Figure 24.

After the external factors affecting each function have been identified, a combined list is drawn, redundancies are eliminated, and definitions are sharpened. In every case, we insist that every trend identified must directly affect the business, whether the effect is positive or negative. It is important to note, however, that external

---

Categories of Long-Run Trends for Use in Identifying External Factors

1. Technical
   Rate of technical progress in
   • New scientific discoveries
   • New substitute technologies
   • New materials
   • New manufacturing processes

2. Economic
   • Changing costs of labor, materials, capital, transportation, energy, taxes, etc.
   • Changing rates of economic development
   • Changing international value of the dollar

3. Social
   • Changing status and role of women
   • Changing lifestyles affecting marriage and family, dress, appearance, diet
   • Changing importance of work ethic

4. Demographic
   • Changing population growth rates and age composition of youth, young adults, seniors, races, etc.
   • Regional shifts in population

5. Political Changes In
   • Regulation and controls
   • Product liability
   • Environmental protection
   • Welfare
   • Medical care
   • Military readiness
   • Foreign travel and tariff agreements

Figure 24

factors and long-run trends are not, in themselves, inherently positive or negative. The same trend in democratization of the former Soviet Union may be positive for opportunities in oil exploration and negative for development of new advanced fighter aircraft.

A good example occurred when a general aviation manufacturing company went to work to develop opportunity selection criteria. After defining product-markets and identifying strengths, weaknesses, and long-run trends, it became clear that there were a number of long-run trends that did not bode well for one of its major product markets—single-engine aircraft for personal training, transportation, and enjoyment purchased by individuals through distributors in the United States. Three of the trends identified were: (1) increasing costs of ownership caused by increasing costs of product liability, increased amount of instrumentation required, and rising fuel costs; (2) more government control of air traffic because of increasing amounts of air traffic, especially near population centers; and (3) higher levels of professional piloting skills required to operate aircraft in the modern controlled environment.

To a pilot whose primary interest in flying is the enjoyment of feeling free, all of these trends tend to reduce the fun. One such pilot told us that the F.A.A. is like the "Grinch who stole the fun out of flying." Another member of a flying club objected to the purchase of a transponder for the club's plane (which would make it more visible on radar and report its altitude) because he didn't want "Big Brother" watching him all the time while he flew.

Although these three trends might be considered negative ones for the single-engine, recreational-use, owner-flown product market, the same trends were positive (or at least not negative) for the product-market for medium-size jet aircraft flown by professional pilots for transportation of executives of corporations in the United States. Although other factors were involved, it is not surprising that the sale of new corporate jet aircraft has grown dramatically during the past decade, while sales of new small single-engine aircraft declined to historically low levels.

Fortunately for the industry, the end of the Cold War signaled an end to (or reduction in) the supply of professional pilots for airlines and corporations entirely trained by the military. Thus, the need for additional training of professional pilots can be expected to increase the demand somewhat for single-engine aircraft to be used in training operations.

The primary purpose of identifying external factors and long-run trends is to aid in selecting opportunities that are supported by long-run trends, rather than having to buck trends. Going with the flow of two or more positive trends is like riding the crest of a wave. The only effort required is to keep going in the right direction to benefit from the force of the wave. On the other hand, bucking negative trends is like swimming against the tide or swimming upstream. It's good for conditioning, but it's hard to make much headway.

The Mental Work Required Is Well Worth the Effort

Opportunity selection criteria can be a powerful tool in stimulating creativity in an organization and providing guidance in the selection of opportunities that can contribute synergistically to a firm's overall growth and profits over time. But this happens only when management takes the time and devotes the mental effort to think though the issues involved in framing the selection criteria.

Unfortunately, management is sometimes reluctant to devote the time and mental energy that, one executive remarked, "can really make your head hurt." However, without the effort, selection criteria can be ineffective and can send confusing signals to others in the organization. Done properly, the result is well worth the effort, leading to success both tactically and strategically.

9

The Power of Scientific Thought Process in New Product Opportunity Analysis

Every new product opportunity for a given firm is like a giant puzzle to be solved. Some puzzles are more complex and difficult, but all have the same structure and/or components. The key to successful opportunity analysis is to accomplish the tasks of defining, evaluating, and determining total requirements in a manner that solves the puzzle (regarding a new product opportunity) both quickly and efficiently.

This can be accomplished with logical, sequential decisions that define and resolve the critical issues at each step in the evaluation process. A critical issue can be defined as the presence or absence of any factor (piece of the puzzle) that would make or break the opportunity. The result is a branching network of decisions, each depending on the outcome of the previous ones. Our approach always maintains focus on obtaining the most relevant information at each step in the sequence, with minimum time and effort. It is possible that the resulting "decision tree" could be different for every new product development activity, although we have found certain sequences that always yield fast, clean results.

Attention is focused on achieving understanding in sufficient depth on each issue (at each branch) to make clear decisions without major mistakes. This does not mean that a detailed solution to each issue must be achieved before progressing to other steps. It means only that sufficient information (understanding) is obtained at that point to either resolve the issue completely or ascertain that the issue can be resolved within the time and resource constraints, so that additional activities may be initiated without fear of wasting time or resources.

For example, a critical issue in the development of plastic instrument panels for automobiles was whether a plastic material could meet the combined requirements for safety in crashes, heat resistance, and color stability within the value/cost constraints imposed by automotive manufacturers. Once the physical and economic requirements were established, research scientists were able to determine quickly from laboratory experiments that such a material could be developed from a combination of engineering thermoplastics and existing ABS plastic materials. Although the new material was not yet perfected, the issue was resolved to the extent that management could proceed in confidence with other aspects of the product development process.

Our process is best characterized as a disciplined method of inquiry, guided by framing hypotheses that provide initial focus on issues critical to the success of the proposed new product innovation. The method also employs multiple alternative hypotheses of cause-effect, which lead to fast, clean decisions. Research design, data collection, and analysis employ a variety of techniques depending on the nature of the information needed and its sources.

The key is to collect whatever data are necessary by whatever method is most efficient to test the hypotheses to establish a firm knowledge base of understanding, and then to build on that understanding as the problem-solving process continues. This method of researching for understanding is perhaps best characterized by the legendary detective work of Sherlock Holmes or that portrayed on TV by Peter Falk in his role of "Columbo." It is also similar to good investigative reporting or to the field work of a paleontologist or Egyptologist searching to understand the past. Such research is usually guided by well-founded hypotheses, based on a previous collection of knowledge or facts, which may be expressed as a conceptual model.

The data-gathering skills and tools required are often a mixture of those of clinical psychologists and the disciplined thought processes of early scientists like Michael Faraday, Louis Pasteur, and Francis Bacon, whose similar scientific reasoning processes enabled them to solve early mysteries of electricity, infectious disease, and food preservation. Our method is remarkably similar to that used successfully by these early scientists. Because it is largely overlooked by modern-day scientists, the astonishing power of this earlier reasoning process often goes unappreciated.

The Technique of Strong Inference

John R. Platt, professor of biophysics and physics at the University of Chicago, calls this method of reasoning the "technique of strong inference." He explains that the two greatest contributions to development of this method came from Francis Bacon, who pioneered the use of conditional induction trees, which proceeded from alternative hypotheses to experiments (data gathering) to exclude alternatives which led to the adoption of other hypotheses; and Thomas Chamberlain, a geologist at the University of Chicago at the turn of the century, who advocated a "method of multiple hypotheses" to round out the earlier Baconian scheme and to avoid the troubles of the single hypothesis approach.[12]

The problem with the single hypothesis is that one tends to become attached to it, leading to an almost unconscious pressing of the theory to make it fit the facts and pressing of the facts to make them fit the theory. If this can happen in the halls of science, it is easy to see how it can happen in business when overzealous new-product champions distort or overlook facts to support their (single) product idea! But the power of the technique of strong inference is not only in preventing mistakes; it is also in the speed with which it resolves complex problems or issues.

The speed in resolving these issues is more a result of method than of greater knowledge or rare gifts of genius. For example, in Pasteur's time, there were experts who knew much more about the major biological diseases of that period than he did. Yet, using a different method of reasoning, Pasteur was able, every two or three years, to solve one major problem after another from fermentation of beet sugar to diseases of silk worms, anthrax in sheep, and rabies.

His success was obviously not simply a result of luck or greater knowledge, but of the power of a different method. Likewise, it is not our encyclopedic knowledge that has produced success after success with new product innovation in diverse fields. Nor has it been simply luck. It comes from applying the systematic power of the scientific thought process.

The power is derived from two principal features: (1) well-conceived models that enable the researcher to identify and focus the research efforts on critical issues in early stages of the development process; and (2) the use of multiple alternative hypotheses. The result is the ability to cleanly reject some hypotheses, while accepting others. The hypotheses may relate to specific user requirements in the target market, or to bases for competitive advantage, or feasibility of technical alternatives.

When developing products for industrial/commercial and aerospace/defense product-markets, it is not uncommon to resolve all critical issues and provide immediate guidance to many subsequent development activities with only a few (three to six) well-chosen field interviews conducted by a person having sound technical knowledge of the subject. Critical issues regarding unmet needs or technical requirements often can be resolved in one or two interviews, or with a few hours of experimental research in the laboratory.

One such executive, a technically-trained president of a large aerospace firm with years of experience with Planned Innovation, comments:

> In order to increase the number of opportunities a resources-limited group can evaluate, we performed the so-called "Chicken Test" right at the beginning of the preliminary research phase. We borrowed the name from the aircraft jet engine guys. Their lesson, learned the hard way over many years, says that, independent of all the great performance parameters you have designed and verified through tests, you don't have anything if you can't shoot a chicken into a running engine without the compressor or other pieces exploding. It became obvious to perform the

Chicken Test as early as possible. In other words, find the most crucial no-go criteria right at the beginning and start the preliminary research by validating them. If you verified the no-go, you saved yourself lots of time which could be used to go after a better opportunity. Needless to say, the Chicken Test works great in my private life, for evaluating investment opportunities, for example.

One example in which we were involved focused on evaluating the feasibility of developing an automatic guidance system for large coal mining boring machines. An initial critical issue was whether safety considerations would permit the operation of such unmanned equipment in coal mines. Despite the fact that equipment manufacturers were very positive on the issue, the opportunity analyst chose to investigate it by talking to key personnel at the U.S. Bureau of Mines. The analyst quickly learned that the simplest of equipment, even light bulbs, took months to years of safety testing before being approved for use in mines. Automatically guided boring equipment, which would create a large tunnel in a mine, would most likely be subject to breakdowns requiring human intervention for repairs. The resulting costs of safety requirements would easily negate the advantages of automatic guidance. All critical issues were resolved decisively in a total of three interviews.

Although AMF had a major share of the bowling industry during the 1980s, it was not achieving success with sales of bowling balls. Hypothesizing that there was something technically wrong, analysts interviewed a few expert professional bowlers who had tried the ball. They all replied that they simply could not throw strikes consistently with the ball. This led AMF researchers to investigate the technical requirements for consistently obtaining the correct trajectory (with the correct hook at the end). The research (on many possible causes) ultimately resulted in the introduction of the urethane coating on the exterior of the ball which enabled it to perform exactly as required.

The new ball (called the "Angle") was an immediate success in the hands of both professionals and amateurs, and sales and profits increased sharply, restoring its desired market share. This initial success in the redesign of bowling balls sparked industry-wide research leading to present-day resin-coated balls that perform even better. These new balls have made it possible for bowlers to roll consistently higher scores, leading to greater enjoyment of the sport and continued economic health of the whole industry.

In another case, a manufacturer of industrial circuit breakers was investigating the (hypothesized) unmet need for a lower-cost computer circuit breaker at the request of a purchasing agent in the computer company. To understand the technical requirements for the breaker and the feasibility of a lower-cost alternative, the analyst went directly to the company and interviewed the project engineer in charge of the product. While they were reviewing the electrical diagram involving the circuit breaker, the opportunity analyst, also an electronic engineer, noticed that the same circuit was protected by a low-cost diode. When asked why both protection devices were necessary, the project engineer suddenly recalled that they had substituted the low-cost diode for the circuit breaker several months back, but had not updated the manufacturing drawing or bill of material sent to purchasing. There was no unmet need. The hypothesis was rejected clearly and decisively with one visit.

These are neither exceptional nor isolated examples. They are the typical result of a logical, disciplined thought process that begins by identifying critical issues and testing to see if the hypothesis is supported or rejected by achieving in-depth understanding directly from the most knowledgeable source.

The Benefit of Hypotheses of Cause-Effect

Two basic types of hypotheses are used in all forms of research. These are: (1) the hypothesis of fact, and (2) the hypothesis of cause-effect.

Hypotheses of fact state that something is, in fact, true, such as "all Caterpillar tractors require hoses that have high reliability and long life." This hypothesis can be tested by contacting a sample of users and obtaining information, which may either support or not support the hypothesis.

The same hypothesis of fact could be extended to a hypothesis of cause-effect by adding one or more "because" statements, as follows: "All Caterpillar tractors require hoses that have high reliability and long life *because* they must operate in severe environments of dust, heat, rain, cold, and snow; and *because* the geographical environments in which they operate often include remote regions where replacement of broken hoses is very costly because of the difficulty of replacing hoses in the field under extreme weather conditions without proper equipment."

These two examples show that the hypothesis of fact, the only focus of the first statement, would be tested automatically as a byproduct of obtaining the greater depth of information needed to test the second hypothesis. Furthermore, when the hypothesis of fact is tested as part of a cause-effect hypothesis using our four-question sequence, the result contains a richness of understanding that far surpasses that attained with hypothesis of fact alone. The requirements research guided by the second hypothesis would address:

1. What degree of reliability and life are obtained now under different environmental conditions and geographic locations?
2. What does it cost to maintain equipment now, including cost of maintenance personnel, spare parts and equipment, and opportunity cost caused by down-time (is there loss of emotive value due to down-time)?
3. What improvements are needed in reliability and/or methods of repair?
4. What dollar amount (value) can be attached to maintaining reliability under varying conditions and in different geographical areas (are there emotive as well as economic sources of value)?

The larger amount of information required in the second cause-effect hypothesis can usually be obtained with very little additional marginal costs. In essence, the power of our scientific methodology is built into the research process, and a wealth of valuable understanding is gained at very little additional cost. The net result is a great bargain because the hypotheses also have other beneficial effects throughout the new product development process, as summarized in Figure 25.

Besides guiding the research process, the hypotheses lead to the

---

The Value of Hypotheses in Opportunity Analysis

1. Guide research process

2. Discipline thought process and lead to collection of essential information only

3. Ensure coverage of all relevant aspects when used with the Planned Innovation Model

4. Help preserve objectivity of all involved

5. Prevent misunderstanding–understanding changes (shifts) during research process

6. Preserve reasoning process over time (document increase in understanding)

7. Help organize and relate diverse information to logical findings and conclusions

8. Help organize report writing

Figure 25

collection of essential information only, while assuring that all necessary aspects are covered. In researching new product opportunities, there are many items of information that might be interesting, but are not absolutely essential to the particular stage of the decision process. This is especially true in early phases of the investigation where one can become fascinated with details, such as whether the display should have green or red lights, before it has been decided that a visual display will be needed. Without the necessary discipline that stems from the hypothesis-testing process, the research can be exhaustive, consume valuable time, and cost far too much.

The hypothesis-testing process also helps preserve the objectivity of all persons or departments involved by documenting the level of understanding existing at various stages of the research process. Writing it down prevents misunderstandings that otherwise invariably result. The time frame involved in some new product developments can span several years or longer. Key managers get promoted, and new personnel have no way to learn what the reasoning process was several years ago when the project was started. But even without shifts in personnel, as knowledge grows over time from the investigations underway, viewpoints about the market need, technological alternatives, or competition almost certainly change. To keep the logical decision process on track, one needs to be able to look back to a year (or month) before and review just what the reasoning process was at the beginning, before new information began coloring the situation. In preserving harmonious working relationships among the various departments involved, it is valuable to be able to review the original technical, marketing, competitive, and possible manufacturing cost assumptions that led to the initiation of the project in the first place. What appears today to be an uneconomical approach or an approach to an inadequate market may have been a perfectly logical approach a few years or months before.

Finally, the hypothesis-testing process helps to organize the diverse informational inputs for preparing research reports. It also provides a check that all pertinent information has indeed been obtained. Even though drafting hypotheses is often considered an awkward chore at first, our experience has shown that, within a few weeks, personnel become skilled and comfortable with the task.

Scientifically Based Opportunity Analysis Can Be Valuable at Any Stage of New Product Development

Over the years, we have entered the scene of new product activities at every conceivable stage in the process with many firms while serving in the role of teachers and "coaches." We have seen situations driven by new technological discoveries without specific ideas of where or how the discoveries could be put to commercial use. This situation happens frequently as the result of fundamental research programs in large firms producing basic materials such as chemicals, plastics, and glass. But unexpected discoveries can occur in any size or type of firm. Often a technology developed for one purpose can find unanticipated use in other applications. The same model and scientific reasoning process is useful in these situations, although the process may not lead to a solution as swiftly as it does when initiated by recognition of an unmet market need for which a new technical solution is required.

We have also been involved at the very beginning of the recognition of an unmet need with high value in a potential market where there was almost no idea of what kind of product, using what technology, would be appropriate to solve the problem and become a commercial success. This happened with the development of gym mats for the American Athletics Division of AMF (now a separate company, American Athletics, Inc.). While searching for ways to rejuvenate a mature gymnastics equipment business, the firm discovered that the canvas-covered gym mats were restricting the amount of time gymnasts could practice in preparation for an upcoming Olympics. Athletes were getting shin-splints after practicing for as little as thirty minutes.

Although the firm had no preconceived ideas about how the problem could be solved, it began a systematic study of physical, economic, and technical requirements that led ultimately to the development of mats with the correct properties. They found that it was possible for another company, Dow Chemical, to formulate ethafoam plastic to meet their special requirements. The resulting new product contributed significantly to the success of U.S. gymnasts in those Olympics, and became the standard for gymnasiums throughout the world—a truly successful innovation.

The generic usefulness of our scientifically based reasoning process was expressed by a European business manager who had received training in opportunity analysis earlier in his career:

> I have worked as a business developer in plastics, and more recently in the energy industry. In my commercial management assignments, I have found that the discipline of the Planned Innovation methodology can be borrowed for purposes as diverse as screening power projects by size and geography, evaluating the "fit" of a potential energy management business acquisition, and determining one business's optimum role in a plastics recycling venture. The concepts of *customer need, match of resources, competitive opening and advantage,* for example, were all helpful in focusing my analysis of these opportunities.

A major "unsolved mystery" regarding a new product innovation is often the motivator for top management to search for improved methods to guide new product development activities. We have served as detectives in situations involving a wide range of products for different markets, such as electro-optical gauging equipment, solar energy systems, computer terminals and other peripherals, gyroscopic instruments, bakery equipment, gas separation equipment, and various component materials and parts, to mention a few. We came to call this part of our work "Red Adair" assignments, based on the legendary success of Red Adair in putting out oil well fires.

Using the scientific thought process guided by the our model, together with our four framework questions, we were able to quickly identify the cause of trouble in many diverse situations in order to "stop the bleeding" and resolve the problem.

10

Opportunity Analysis: Initial Assessment Phase

The initial assessment phase of Opportunity Analysis, the first of three phases, has proven to be a most valuable and powerful phase of analysis. In many instances, it is the only analysis required. This is especially true with modifications and extensions of existing products, where only a few key items of information are needed to evaluate and guide the necessary product innovation. On the other hand, major product modifications and new products developed for new markets will usually also require one or two additional phases—range of requirements and quantitative confirmation of market potential. A summary of the activities in the initial phase is presented in Figure 26.

Most new product development activities involve modifications and extensions of existing products for existing or new markets. And well they should, because our experience has shown that these activities require obtaining only a small amount of information and entail the lowest risk.

As shown in the Figure 27, modification of existing products for new markets requires more information and entails greater risk than modifications for existing markets, and development of new products for new markets requires an even greater amount of information and entails the greatest risk, because there are more unknowns and critical issues to resolve successfully, especially in the market domain.

Initial Assessment

PURPOSE
To Ensure
- That there is an unmet need of sufficient value to users
- That all critical issues can be resolved
- That there are no major obstacles to success, and that there is ample reason to believe that success can be achieved

FOCUS OF HYPOTHESIS
- Is there an unmet market need of sufficient value to the users?
- Can all critical issues be resolved?
- Is there a match of company (division) resources to opportunity, or at least no totally disqualifying mismatch?
  - QUALITATIVE: Can the company handle the technology, production, marketing, and financing
  - QUANTITATIVE: Is the market large enough, or too large, to meet the opportunity selection criteria?
- Is there a reasonable basis for competitive opening and competitive advantage?
- Check any doubtful aspect regarding opportunity selection criteria, including external long-range trends.

PROCEDURE
- Define the opportunity.
- Verify that opportunity meets selection criteria and establish priority.
- Identify critical issues.
- Formulate hypotheses based on critical issues.
- Determine information needed to test hypotheses.
- Identify few (three to ten) knowledgeable, cooperative users (who can provide information needed).
- Use nonstructured personal interview, guided by hypotheses and four framework questions.

OUTPUT
- Does opportunity warrant proceeding with development or, at least, with further evaluation?

CONCLUSION
- Decide whether to discontinue, establish priority for development, or to proceed to determine range of variation in requirements (phase two).

TIME AND EFFORT
- Three to six weeks and 120 to 320 man-hours.

Figure 26

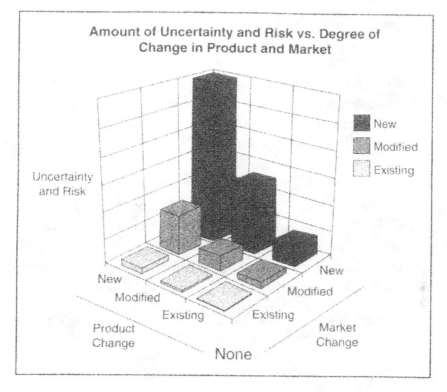

Figure 27

It has been our experience that approximately eighty percent of potential new product problems and issues can be resolved in the initial assessment phase. This phase prevents major mistakes by disclosing critical weaknesses, and provides guidance by clearly indicating the best choices among various product design, manufacturing, and marketing alternatives. Very often, the definition of requirements achieved in this phase alone is sufficient to provide direction to other functional departments, with little or no additional special research efforts needed beyond that required in normal departmental routines.

First, Define the Opportunity

It is sometimes amazing to see how far new product development activities have proceeded without any clear idea of where they are going. This happens often in technology-driven firms, where management tacitly assumes that any improvements or advances in technology associated with existing products will somehow be useful. But it also happens frequently when completely new products are being developed for new markets. In that instance, the excuse is usually that it is not yet clear exactly where the product is going. Both of these scenarios are invitations to disaster or, at least, a very inefficient use of resources.

Regardless of how the opportunity originates (technology driven or market-needs driven) or where it is in the total development process (from idea recognition to market introduction), the process will proceed in an inefficient or out-of-control manner unless the opportunity has been clearly defined *in writing*. We recommend that the definitional format be based on the following concepts:

1. Functional Product-Market Definition
2. Opportunity Selection Criteria
3. Our Models of Requirements for Successful Innovation and Basis of Value

Content from these concepts is combined in Figure 28 to show a suggested format for opportunity definition.

Ideas for new products or modifications of existing products need to be encouraged and solicited from everyone within a firm, preferably guided by opportunity selection criteria. In order to encourage a free flow of ideas, we do not feel the initial statement of the idea should conform to a specific format. There needs to be only enough information to understand what is being suggested.

The first step in the initial assessment is to clarify and more precisely define the idea. The information should be obtained (and recorded) by a trained opportunity analyst, using readily available sources within the firm, starting with the person who suggested the idea.

There is a purpose for every item in the outline. First, the four-part functional product-market concept provides an immediate market orientation. This is especially valuable if the new opportunity originated from a technical discovery and not from recognition of an unmet market need. Note that the four-part definition starts with

---

Format for Opportunity Definition

Define Functional Product-Market
- Functional Needs (to do what)
- Product Type (what general product)
- Customer (for whom)
- Geography (where)

Compare With Selection Criteria: Indicate how the opportunity
- Will meet business strategic and tactical objectives re:
  - Preferred kind of product-markets?
  - Desired amount of sales and profitability?
- Will match resources re:
  - Key capabilities (strengths) to be used?
  - Economy of scale in sales, R&D and investment?
  - Provide competitive opening and advantage?
    - Names of anticipated major competitors
  - Be reinforced by favorable external factors and long-range trends without bucking any?

Identify Unmet Need re:
- How is functional need being done (met) now?
- What does present method cost now? What is the approximate basis of total value now; percentage of economic versus emotive?
- What is wrong (not being met) with present method?
- What would be value of (suggested) improvements to method (amount and source)? What would be the approximate basis of additional value; percentage of economic versus emotive?

Figure 28

functional needs rather than with product, since the product is not yet defined as a market-oriented approach to a new product innovation (whereas with existing businesses, the product already exists). We must start by examining which functions, having what value to the customer, need to be performed, and then decide what type of product can be developed to meet those needs. The functional product-market concept also places focus on who the customers (users) will be and where they are geographically located. This provides an early hypothesis regarding the target market to whom the whole effort is directed, again reinforcing a market orientation.

The second part of the definition is intended to ensure that the opportunity is consistent with the firm's opportunity selection criteria.

No new product development activity should be started or be allowed to continue if its purpose is inconsistent with carefully conceived selection criteria.

The third part of the definition reflects the universal criterion that any desirable new product opportunity will address an unmet need (or problem) of sufficient value to the customers (users) to make it worthwhile to pursue. The immediate output from the whole definitional process becomes the input for defining hypotheses to guide subsequent stages of analysis and assessment.

What should be done if the answers to these questions are not known and, therefore, cannot be obtained from readily available sources within the firm? Actually, all the information needed to complete the outline is seldom available. The outline is designed to disclose at the earliest possible time what is and is not known about the requirements for success for the new opportunity. Enough must eventually become known to determine that the potential opportunity is consistent with the firm's opportunity selection criteria. Beyond that, the initial unknowns merely determine the critical issues to be examined in the next stages of the evaluation process.

Second, Verify that Opportunity Meets Selection Criteria and Establish Priority

In the normal sequence of events, a new product idea will first be identified, hopefully with the opportunity selection criteria already providing direction; defined by an analyst, using readily available information as just described; reviewed to ascertain that it does match the opportunity selection criteria; and, if so, given priority for evaluation and development, along with other new product opportunities that may compete for the same resources. After being chosen for evaluation, the assessment process would continue with the identification of critical issues and conduct of other research activities.

In this normal sequence, using the opportunity selection criteria with well-defined opportunities, it is possible to achieve a three-way classification of opportunities with reasonable accuracy, as shown in Figure 29.

Output from Opportunity Selection Criteria
(When Used With Well-Defined Opportunities)

THE OPPORTUNITY

1. Definitely meets selection criteria and should be further evaluated

2. Definitely does not meet selection criteria (usually because of serious misalignment with objectives or mismatch of resources) and should not be evaluated at this time

3. Partially meets selection criteria, but it is questionable whether opportunity should be pursued at this time

---

Figure 29

This three-way classification provides an initial priority. We recommend that no opportunities be totally rejected—only that they not be given priority for attention at this time. If the opportunity does not provide a match to existing resources, but is needed to implement an important strategic move, then a program involving acquisition is more appropriate than internal development alone. Conditions also change over time, especially technological factors, market conditions, and competition. An opportunity that is questionable today could become attractive in a year or two.

Modification and extension of existing products may get started as part of day-to-day operations and then grow into major products eating up precious time and resources which could be better allocated to other projects. This happens frequently when central research and development organizations are given a budget without clear direction as to which products to develop.

We have found numerous instances where only a few out of many existing projects really made sense in terms of the (newly established) opportunity selection criteria. In such cases, shifting resources from the opportunities that definitely did not meet the criteria to the few that positively did meet the criteria always produced dramatic results in terms of increased output from the lab and, ultimately, increased sales and profits.

We have learned from these experiences that all new product development activities, beyond a very minimal level of effort and cost, should be defined, reviewed, and prioritized with the selection criteria, and then further evaluated. Though it may sound cumbersome and formal to insist on establishing this discipline, it quickly pays off in increased growth and profits for the business.

Third, Identify Critical Issues

Because the presence of an unmet need with sufficient value to the user is always an absolute requirement for success, and is almost always not understood in sufficient depth, unmet needs are always considered critical issues. Often, the definition of customers as part of the functional product-market definition is a critical issue because of its close association with understanding unmet needs and value, which in turn translates into amount of sales (forecasts) needed for appropriate matching of resources to the opportunity. Frequently, the bases for competitive opening and advantage are also critical, as are the anticipated effects of external factors and long-range trends.

The initial consideration of all factors critical to success establishes the research hypotheses and determines the sequence of information-gathering activities for the steps that follow. This logical process, which results in the narrowing of focus to a few critical issues, is one key to achieving speed and efficiency in opportunity analysis. Further efficiency is achieved by the type of research procedures followed.

Important connections exist between the suggested format for opportunity definition and the resulting identification of critical issues. The critical issues become the bases for initial framing of hypotheses because they give expression to the information most needed to resolve uncertainty regarding the requirements for (possible) success of the opportunity.

Fourth, Formulate Hypotheses Based on Critical Issues

The statement of hypotheses to guide opportunity analysis is actually relatively simple and straightforward. Yet, it seems to strike fear in the minds of management, and even in researchers who have not been disciplined to write down their hypotheses before beginning the research process. This apprehension is often based on the misconception that, by framing any hypothesis, they are disclosing their ignorance and/or exposing themselves to possible embarrassment later when it is discovered to be unsupportable.

This is akin to the other problems inherent in the single-hypothesis approach to research. To avoid embarrassment, the executive or researcher tries to collect and interpret all data to support the hypothesis, and to overlook any data to the contrary. The problem can be avoided completely with the scientific approach, using multiple alternative hypotheses. With a scientific approach, the focus is on finding the truth of the situation, whatever it is, so that correct understanding is attained.

This approach positions the role of hypotheses to one of guiding the inquiry in a logical manner. Hypotheses are never right or wrong, anyway, only supported or not supported by the evidence. The approach also places emphasis on defining exactly what evidence would clarify the issues, leading to which hypotheses should be rejected, and, therefore, which accepted. The central focus on finding the truth is strengthened by using the four-question sequence to obtain information to test hypotheses objectively by always starting with:

1. How is it done now?
2. What does it cost now?
3. What is wrong with present solutions?
4. What is the potential value associated with improvements?

This approach places emphasis on first establishing a base of understanding through use of the first two questions, and then proceeding to build on that base with the third and fourth questions.

Fifth, Determine What Information Would Provide the Most Decisive Test of Hypotheses

The most decisive test of any set of hypotheses is achieved by obtaining information which clearly signals rejection of one hypothesis, and supports acceptance of the alternative. Although the concepts underlying statistical tests of hypotheses are useful in identifying information needed in testing the initial critical hypotheses regarding new product opportunities, it is seldom necessary to employ statistical sampling or formal research designs. Usually all one need do is to take time to think or reason about what information, obtained from whom, or by what engineering or laboratory tests, would be conclusive in rejecting the hypothesis, then use the four-question sequence to obtain the information.

When using statistical (random) sampling techniques, the power of the test is increased by increasing the sample size. Our procedures are able to achieve an equivalent power of the test with much smaller sample sizes than in random sampling because much more relevant information is obtained per sample.

To verify this subjective measure, all one would have to do in each case is to ask management to estimate the probability that a mistake was made. The answer in all the cases cited would be "practically zero." Recall the examples of the new gym mats and solid-state crash-survivable flight data recorders. In both cases the unmet need and value were verified conclusively by means of a few well-chosen interviews. The alternative hypothesis, that there was neither unmet need nor value, was rejected. It makes no difference whether the hypothesis is stated in the positive or negative form. The hypothesis guides the inquiry to the truth of the situation and that is the ultimate objective. Note also that identifying the information needed to test hypotheses and determining how to get the information, or from whom, are closely related. Herein lies another key to speed and efficiency.

Sixth, Go for the Jugular in Obtaining Information

We have found situations where researchers were essentially beating around the bush or taking elaborate roundabout approaches in testing hypotheses regarding new product opportunities. It seemed they were either afraid of finding out the truth of the situation or they were making a small career out of the job. These experiences led us to advocate that opportunity analysts should always seek the quickest, most direct approach to information needed to test hypotheses. We nicknamed this practice "going for the jugular." The object is to achieve a quick kill (of the hypothesis) like a cheetah downing a gazelle, or to rejoice in finding the answer quickly and efficiently.

A surefire way of achieving this objective would be simply to find someone who knows and ask him or her. This person must also understand in depth why the answer is whatever it is. And, to achieve the depth of understanding required, the interviewer must have the ability to communicate with this person to discuss issues in sufficient detail. This often requires that the interviewer has sufficient depth of technical or other specialized knowledge.

Of course, it is very possible that the person or group with the greatest understanding is not willing to discuss the subject with the interviewer. Therefore, another selection criterion is needed; the person or group must see potential benefit from the information exchange. Since the critical issues almost always require in-depth understanding of user needs, the problem is one of finding potential customers who are knowledgeable and cooperative. Such users can be often identified by mentally addressing the thought-provoking questions, "Who (which customer, user, etc.) would realize the greatest benefit from the proposed new product concept? Who has the greatest problem or need for the proposed product?"

Fortunately, the user, firm, or military unit that has the greatest need would also realize the greatest value and, furthermore, usually has the greatest depth of understanding of the requirements to meet the need. Recall that the development of solid-state crash-survivable flight data recorders was triggered by the (valuable) need to understand why F-16 fighter aircraft were crashing. The value of improved hull designs by AMF for catamarans was greatest for the U.S. participants in the Little America's Cup race, who also understood that a small increase in speed would make the difference between winning or losing this prestigious race. The same was true in the development of gymnasium mats, developed originally for U.S. Olympic athletes.

If the analyst starts with the question of who has the greatest need and value (and understanding) for the product, and then proceeds directly to tapping the information (going for the jugular) from that source, the chances of success are very good. And, if success is not achieved with the first potential source, that source is usually able to suggest a better one. In this way, the investigation being guided by the search for understanding is able to home in quickly on the best sources.

Seldom does the process require more than three tries to locate a suitable, knowledgeable, cooperative source who can provide some decisive information and lead to others as well. A total of three to six interviews is typical for the assessment of critical issues, with as many as ten interviews required only in exceptional circumstances.

What Should Be Accomplished in the Initial Assessment Phase

The ultimate objective of the initial assessment phase is to ensure that there are no major obstacles to success with the proposed new product innovation. Moreover, enough understanding has been obtained to resolve all critical issues and achieve positive verification of an unmet need of sufficient value in at least one to three potential product-markets. The net result is the conclusion that the firm is very unlikely to make a major mistake if it proceeds with the development and, therefore, very likely to succeed, even though every detail of all requirements has not been defined. The result is achieved by meeting the eight criteria shown in Figure 30.

The basic requirement is that research should not proceed to the next phases until all criteria have been met. If the main objective of the initial assessment phase is not met, the firm will be unable to proceed confidently without the risk of making a major mistake. The initial base of understanding simply has not been established on which to build the next level. When the initial assessment phase has been accomplished, the necessary base of understanding has been established to design the next phase of research and formulate the more specific, detailed hypotheses regarding the range of requirements in different product-market segments. If the new product opportunity involves only a modification or extension of an existing product for a familiar product-market, it may not be necessary to complete the remaining phases. In a high percentage of such cases, and even in some instances where a new product is being developed for familiar product-markets, all critical issues are resolved by the

---

Criteria for Completing Initial Assessment Phase

1. Direct Positive confirmation of need (met and unmet) by talking with user having need, not based on secondhand information.

2. Satisfactory answers to all four framework questions about unmet market need and value in some product-market segments.

3. Identification of sources of value, including approximate mix of basis of economic and emotive value with adequate understanding to calculate approximate values in dollar terms.

4. Establish reasonable basis that product-market potential is (or will be) at least large enough to meet minimum sales criteria.

5. Determination that there is no totally disqualifying mismatch of resources to the opportunity that would preclude internal development. (If such disqualifying mismatch is found the assessment should indicate whether or not it is clearly feasible to overcome mismatch via acquisition, joint venture, or licensing.)

6. Identification of reasonable basis for competitive opening and advantage.

7. Identification of at least two positive external supporting trends and no negative ones.

8. Any other issues critical to this specific opportunity have been favorably resolved, or it is clear that they can be resolved within the time and resources available.

Figure 30

end of the initial assessment phase. The increased depth of understanding achieved at this point often provides a comfortable basis for proceeding with the development process with no further structured analysis. The remaining steps can be completed as part of normal activities within the functions involved.

If further research and analysis are required, as is almost always the case when a radically different new product is being developed, and particularly when it is for a new product-market, the opportunity analyst should not be tempted to move on to the next phase before all the criteria listed in Figure 30 are met.

11

Opportunity Analysis:
Range of Requirements Phase

During the initial assessment phase, attention is directed toward one or very few product-market segments. Interviews are sought with users who have the greatest need because they will probably receive the greatest value from the proposed product and because they also tend to have the best understanding of requirements to meet the need. This narrow product-market focus enables the opportunity analyst to determine quickly if there is an unmet need of sufficient value to the user, to resolve critical issues, and meet the other limited objectives. If the understanding gained is sufficient to conclude that there is no unmet need of sufficient value to the user in the segment(s) with greatest need, then there is no reason to examine the remaining segments, saving a great deal of time and effort.

But the narrow focus does not provide a balanced view of the market, resources, and competitive requirements needed to serve a full spectrum of potential product-markets. In essence, the initial assessment phase has looked at only one end (the upper end) of a possible spectrum of requirements needed across different product-market segments of possible interest to the firm. A summary of the activities in the range of requirements phase is presented in Figure 31.

Analysis of Range of Requirements

PURPOSE
- To determine range of variation in functional product requirements
  - Physical and nonphysical
  - Economic and emotive value
  - Technical alternatives
- To determine range of resource requirements
  - Production
  - Marketing
  - Financial

- To identify basis for competitive opening and advantage in different production markets
- To identify competitors and characteristics of competitive products in different product markets

FOCUS OF HYPOTHESIS
- To identify range of variation in requirements among major product-market segments of potential interest:
  - Physical and nonphysical
  - Economic and emotive value
  - Technical
  - Production
  - Marketing
  - Financial
  - Competitive opening and advantage

PROCEDURE
- State hypothesis
- Select (non-random) sample of users in potential product-markets, which represent range of variation in requirements
- Use prestructured questionnaire, administered by personal interview
- Interviews may be required at several levels in organization

OUTPUT
- Identification of range of requirements
- Conclusion:
    Product-market requirements are (are not) feasible for company to meet (physical, nonphysical, economic and emotive, technical, production and marketing) in different product-markets.
- Conclusion
    There is (is not) reasonable basis for competitive opening and advantages in different product-markets.

CONCLUSION
- Discontinue or continue to refine quantitative estimate of potential (third phase)

TIME AND EFFORT
- 10 to 20 weeks, with 500 to 2,000 man-hours for industrial/commercial and aerospace/defense products

Figure 31

The major purposes shown in the figure are to determine the range of variation in product and resource requirements, in different segments, to identify the possible bases for the competitive openings and advantage in various segments, and to identify competition and their products in the segments.

Hypotheses now focus the research on identifying the range of variation in requirements. The most important variations are typically found in physical and nonphysical product requirements, and in economic requirements. For example, to meet the needs in some market segments, a new computer may require only a small memory, relatively slow central processing unit (CPU), and slow printer, whereas other segments require larger memories, and faster CPU and printer speeds. Similarly, one market segment may have little displaceable clerical cost, whereas other segments may have large amounts with which to justify the investment in such a computer.

Large variations in physical and economic requirements are often paralleled by variations in technical and production requirements. The slower, lower-cost machine may be able to use a simpler, lower-cost technology, involving state-of-the-art production methods and materials, without the need for special designs and materials, new processes, or tight quality control, compared to that needed for the larger and faster machine. Furthermore, large variations in physical, economic, technical, and production requirements often signal similar variations in financial and marketing resources needed to serve the range of market segments.

The nature and role of hypotheses in this phase can perhaps best be understood by exploring how these hypotheses differ from those in the initial phase. Hypotheses in the initial assessment phase tend to be broad, general statements. The hypotheses regarding physical, nonphysical, and technical requirements are intended merely to ensure that a reasonable match of resources to opportunity will be possible if the new venture is undertaken. On the other hand, to accurately depict the range (of variation) in requirements, hypotheses in the second phase must guide the investigation toward identifying the operational (physical) and technical requirements in sufficient detail to provide meaningful direction for the subsequent R & D effort.

Of course, initial-phase hypotheses can be, and sometimes are, specified in greater detail than is necessary to reach their limited objective. If this is done, it often leads to one of two problems. First, if the project is discontinued after the initial phase, the extra degree of detail has added unnecessary expense to the total product development process. Second, if the project passes the initial stage, there is a tendency to continue into a "quasi–range of requirements" stage without reformulating the hypotheses to the greater degree of specificity required to properly guide the second phase. This almost always leads to an inadequate investigation in the second phase.

Because of the greater level of detail required in the second phase, a larger number of hypotheses is generally needed in comparison to the initial phase. For example, it is common to have three to six major hypotheses in the initial assessment phase and fifteen to twenty in the next phase. To ensure adequate coverage of all requirements, we recommend classifying and grouping hypotheses according to the corner segments of the our model, including physical and nonphysical product requirements, economic and emotive sources of value, technical, manufacturing, marketing, and competitive requirements.

Testing Hypotheses Regarding Range of Requirements

The first step is to select a sample (normally of present or potential customers or users) that represents the range of variation in the target product-market segments to be examined. This need not be a statistically random sample because it is not intended to be an accurate reflection of the size of the markets in each segment. It is chosen to represent the full range of differences expected in all aspects of requirements.

When studying the requirements for automatic labor-time recording in manufacturing plants, the range of requirements depended mainly on the number of employees, the type of pay system (straight hourly, piece rate, incentives), the variations in product manufactured, and the associated method of manufacture (job shop, batch, assembly line). A small plant producing a standard product with a few models mainly for inventory with standard assembly procedures would normally pay its employees on a straight hourly basis, possibly with some group incentive. There would be no need to relate the individual wage to individual piece parts produced because a simple standard cost-accounting system would be adequate for control. This would be an example of the simplest physical and economic requirements, with value based on economic cost savings versus emotive factors.

At the opposite end of the spectrum might be a large producer of special capital equipment. In this case, a large variety of products is produced to order. Job-shop production methods would normally be used, with records required of individual labor time and cost on each operation in the entire manufacturing and assembly process. Some plants of this type employ complex incentive systems as well. The physical requirement to capture labor time is much more extensive, and the value to the user of a successful system is far greater than for the simpler case. An effective labor-time recording system in this environment is the key to greater total efficiency in manufacturing, as well as savings in time-keeper labor.

In researching a product requirement such as this, it is necessary to study several cases of each type in the major target-market segments of interest. Different segments must be investigated to assure that any variation among segments is understood.

Sample Size Required

Variations caused by number and type of users can usually be adequately represented with a total sample size of fifteen to thirty firms. This number is based on experience in researching requirements in industrial/commercial and aerospace/defense product-markets. The range of requirements usually spans three to six product-market segments, and the requirements within each segment can be determined with analysis of user requirements in five or six firms in each segment. However, the total number of interviews required may be two or three times these numbers because several interviews may be required within different functional departments and at different levels within each firm.

We usually start with a target sample of three firms within each hypothetical segment. If, after gaining understanding of requirements within the three firms, it is reasonably clear that firms of this type, size, and geographic area will have similar requirements, we move on to examine another segment whose requirements are hypothesized to be different from the first. Again, the knowledge gained at each step is used to guide the succeeding one.

A successful approach has been first to identify the extremes in requirements and attempt to understand what causes the requirements to vary. Then, additional cases can be selected on a logical basis. Usually, the initial assessment research will provide good insights to determine the most fruitful basis for segmentation and to guide the beginning second phase interviews. After that, the deeper understanding which results from the first few interviews in the second phase is used to guide the next series of investigations. The range of requirements phase is terminated when the additional interviews are no longer disclosing major variations.

Need for a Carefully Structured Questionnaire

A major difference between the initial assessment and range of requirements phases of research involves questionnaire design. Because of the volume and level of detail required in the range of requirements phase, careful structuring of the questionnaire is essential. The researcher must determine precisely what information must be obtained and from whom. The terminology used and data requested must be in the normal language and format used by the respondent.

To get the most accurate and reliable information, it is necessary to obtain each item from the person best qualified to answer. For some items, this may be the general manager of a plant; for others, it may be a machine operator on the production floor.

In studying the requirements for a computer system for small manufacturing firms, ten functional sub-areas were defined and examined for each firm studied. These were: (1) order processing and billing, (2) accounts receivable, (3) purchasing and accounts payable, (4) production control and scheduling, (5) raw material and purchased parts inventory control, (6) finished goods inventory control, (7) payroll, (8) cost accounting, (9) sales analysis, and (10) general accounting. Information needed for each area was first specified and a series of questions was designed for each one. The interview was started by explaining the purpose of the study to the president or general manager and asking three or four general questions. Then the interviewer asked, "May I speak to the person who handles your order processing and billing?" After asking a short series of questions, the interviewer asked to see the person handling accounts receivable, then purchasing and accounts payable, and so forth.

By grouping the questions by functional areas and structuring the questions within each area, an enormous amount of accurate information can be obtained within a relatively short time. Furthermore, no one person within the firm is made to feel as though he or she has been imposed upon. The data processing requirements for the firms in this particular example were completely documented within 1 1/2 to 2 1/2 hours using an eleven-page questionnaire. However, no single person within the firm had to spend more than ten to twenty minutes with the interviewer. An example of the questionnaire used to obtain information regarding the payroll function, requiring only about ten to fifteen minutes to complete, is shown in Figure 32.

The key to obtaining the amount and quality of information needed to determine the product requirements is to carefully structure the questionnaire for ease in responding and to obtain the information from those persons who are most knowledgeable about individual aspects of the total requirements. Although a sample size of fifteen to thirty firms is usually adequate, there may be five to ten short interviews with different individuals within each firm.

It should also be kept in mind that not all aspects of the requirements need to be specified in the same degree of detail. As was the case with hypotheses in the initial assessment phase, only one or two areas usually require detailed investigation. Often, the financial, production, and marketing requirements for a modified product are not significantly different from those of existing products.

Analysis of Competition

The identification of reasonable bases for competitive opening and advantage is always a critical aspect of the initial assessment phase,

Prestructured Questionnaire to Determine
Data Processing Requirements for Payroll Function

RECORD QUESTIONS a THROUGH e IN GRID BELOW

a. Normally, how many people does the company employ in the following categories? What is the maximum number? (READ LIST).

b. How are these groups paid? By salary, hourly rate, incentive pay, or commission, or combination?

c. Are they paid by cash or check?

d. What is the payroll period for each group?

e. How is attendance recorded for payroll?

		Total	Admin. Exec. & Superv.	Clerical	Production	Maintenance	Engin. & Technical	Sales	Other
a. No. in Group									
Average		—	—	—	—	—	—	—	—
Maximum		—	—	—	—	—	—	—	—
b. Type of Payroll (circle)									
Straight Salary		-1	-1	-1	-1	-1	-1	-1	-1
Hourly		-2	-2	-2	-2	-2	-2	-2	-2
Incentive		-3	-3	-3	-3	-3	-3	-3	-3
Hourly & Incentive		-4	-4	-4	-4	-4	-4	-4	-4
Straight Commission		-5	-5	-5	-5	-5	-5	-5	-5
Salary & Commission		-6	-6	-6	-6	-6	-6	-6	-6
		-X	-X	-X	-X	-X	-X	-X	-X
c. Method of Payment									
Cash		-1	-1	-1	-1	-1	-1	-1	-1
Check		-2	-2	-2	-2	-2	-2	-2	-2
		-X	-X	-X	-X	-X	-X	-X	-X
d. Payroll Period									
Day		-1	-1	-1	-1	-1	-1	-1	-1
Week		-2	-2	-2	-2	-2	-2	-2	-2
Two Weeks		-3	-3	-3	-3	-3	-3	-3	-3
Month		-4	-4	-4	-4	-4	-4	-4	-4
Other___ (Specify)		-5	-5	-5	-5	-5	-5	-5	-5
		-X	-X	-X	-X	-X	-X	-X	-X
e. Attendance Record									
None Kept		-1	-1	-1	-1	-1	-1	-1	-1
Time Clock		-2	-2	-2	-2	-2	-2	-2	-2
Other___ (Specify)		-3	-3	-3	-3	-3	-3	-3	-3
		-X	-X	-X	-X	-X	-X	-X	-X

Employee Categories

Figure 32

but the initial assessment is based on only a few product-market segments. It is quite possible that both competitive openings and advantages may differ from product-market segment to segment because competition may vary across the range of segments of interest. During the range of requirements phase, it is important to check the possible range of competitive requirements in greater depth.

The analysis of competition within each product-market segment of interest also provides important information regarding requirements for marketing mixes and associated marketing strategies and plans needed within each segment to succeed against (possibly entrenched) competition. The identification of all major competitors within each segment together with their (approximate) marketing strategies and plans for similar existing products can be considered the ultimate objective.

Obtaining in-depth understanding of competition is seldom wasteful of resources. Most businessmen and women would agree that, "You can't learn too much about your competition." Oddly, though, firms always tend to err in the direction of knowing too little about their competition. In many cases, there seems to be a subconscious aversion to finding out about competitors and their products. That is one of the most important tasks during the second phase.

It is essential that the strengths and weaknesses of existing competitive products be thoroughly understood. An analysis must be made of the characteristics of all major competing products in the product-markets of interest. This often can be done by collecting sales literature and other published information. Present users of competing equipment are usually glad to explain and demonstrate its strong and weak points. They tend to be somewhat biased toward positive attributes, however, because they tend to defend their purchase decision. However, users who are having difficulty with competing equipment are usually very vocal about their problems.

Users are also excellent sources of information concerning price, as well as sales and service support provided by competitors for their products. In general, answers to the question, "What is wrong with existing (competing) equipment?" are a valuable source of information concerning ways to improve and differentiate the new product.

Competitors almost always are strong in certain aspects of their marketing mixes in some product-markets and weak in others. In addition to examining the characteristics of competitive products, it is important to evaluate *their* matching of resources to the opportunity. Valuable information is contained in annual reports, in reports prepared by stock brokerage firms, and from Dun & Bradstreet reports. Often, competing salesmen will tell their customers of plans to introduce new equipment or to delete certain models. Trade shows are also a convenient, excellent source of information on competitive equipment.

The competitive analysis can be a major task when entering new markets for the first time. In this case, it is important to identify where the strongest competition will lie. For example, divisions of large corporations often are not as fiercely competitive as small- or medium-size firms whose whole future depends on a narrow product line. Just because a division of a powerful firm is in the market does not indicate the importance of that market or product line to the parent firm. If the direction of emphasis for the parent corporation has shifted, they may even be willing to sell that division.

We were involved in just such a situation when studying the range of requirements for golf cars (carts) for AMF. A competing manufacturer of a quality golf car was found to be owned by a firm in the insulation and building materials field. In view of the large potential in the firm's primary field, it did not make sense that the firm would devote many resources to the highly competitive golf car field. It came as no surprise when the corporation divested itself of the golf car division a few months after the analysis had been made.

What Should Be Accomplished in the Range of Requirements Phase

A significant level of detail must be reached by the range of requirements analysis to clearly determine whether it is technically feasible to design, manufacture, and market the range of products required within the economic constraints found and the resources of the firm. The analysis must specify the physical, economic, and technical requirements in sufficient detail to be able to guide the R & D effort. This effort should not be initiated until it has been determined which of the various possible product variations should be developed and for which product-market segments. The third phase, quantification of market potential in each segment, is needed to complete this determination.

The conduct of the quantitative confirmation study also depends on the study of range of variation requirements to define the segments and to indicate which persons within the firms to be surveyed have and are willing to provide the necessary information. The in-depth analysis indicated in the range of requirements phase often discloses critical differences in requirements that can determine a more effective segmentation than traditional bases such as Standard Industrial Classification and size of firm. Often, the most valuable segmentation is determined by technology, process, or equipment currently in use, which is disclosed in the range of requirements phase.

The range of requirements survey also discloses the specialized terminology or jargon to use in communicating with respondents and indicates which of several key items of data each respondent will have available and be willing to disclose. Without this input, the quantitative survey either would not be possible at all, or it would not provide the quality of information made possible by the sequential process.

The range of requirements analysis must indicate whether the financial, production, marketing, and management resources are adequate to compete effectively in some or all of the market segments investigated. A clear competitive opening must be identified in each segment of interest, as well as the possible basis for continued protection from competitive reaction.

If it appears feasible to develop some or all of the product variations and to compete effectively in some or all of the product-market segments, the conclusion would be to continue with the third phase, the quantitative confirmation of market potential, in each segment of interest. Otherwise, the project would be discontinued, either permanently or temporarily, depending on the nature of the situation. Often projects that do not proceed immediately to the third phase are put on the shelf to await a specified technological advancement, such as the development of lower-cost computer memories or manufacturing techniques that produce consistently higher-quality components. When the technical advancement occurs, the project is reactivated and reviewed for any changes that might have occurred in the interim. Then, the quantification phase is initiated.

After the successful completion of a range of requirements study, so much information is known about the product, the market, the resource requirements, and the competition that there is a great temptation to proceed immediately with development without the quantitative confirmation of market potential. We have observed several such cases where the temptation was overwhelming to the company. In every case, the economic consequences were undesirable, resulting in much less profit than could have been obtained.

The range of requirements research can be misleading about the relative profitability of different market segments. This second phase is purposely biased to expose the range of possible variation to be faced. What is still needed is an unbiased assessment of the *size* of each product-market segment and the degree of *competitive penetration* and *strength* in each. These factors have a major impact on the ultimate profit to be realized, and thus need quantitative assessment before the total development effort should proceed.

12

Opportunity Analysis: Quantitative Confirmation of Market Potential Phase

There are two main purposes for this third phase—to determine the market potential for possible major design variations in the proposed product and to assess the strength of competition in each of the product-market segments of interest. Activities required in the quantitative confirmation phase are outlined in Figure 33.

This phase is relatively simple and straightforward compared with the range of requirements phase. Traditional market research techniques can be used with superior effectiveness because of the wealth of information now available to design the quantitative research. The time required to complete the research is usually only two to three weeks if estimates can be made from reliable secondary sources and, even if primary survey data is needed, the time and effort are normally only twenty-five to fifty percent of that required for the range of requirements phase.

If this is true, one may wonder why the third phase is not conducted earlier, perhaps along with the second phase. The reason is that the output of the range of requirements phase is necessary to design the quantitative phase. The basis for market segmentation and differences in equipment configuration needed for each segment are a principal output of the preceding range of requirements phase.

Quantitative Confirmation of Market Potential

PURPOSE
- To determine market potential for major design variations in product
- To assess existing competitive market penetration

FOCUS OF HYPOTHESES
- Differences in requirements for various product-market segments
- Sizes of various product-market segments (which have different requirements)
- Existence of competitive equipment in each product-market segment

PROCEDURE
- First, evaluate whether market potentials can be estimated with sufficient accuracy, based on reliable secondary sources. If not, proceed with primary survey:
  - State hypothesis
  - Select random sample (statistical)
  - Stratified by industry or other market segment
  - Short, prestructured questionnaire containing minimum key information on quantity usages, sizes, costs, materials, competitive product used
  - Telephone interview will usually suffice

OUTPUT
- Size of product-market segments (potential) for different product variations
- Penetration of competition in each product-market

CONCLUSION
- Discontinue or proceed with product design and development for selected product-market segments (which will meet all opportunity selection criteria, including sales and profits)

TIME AND EFFORT
- Two to three weeks, and 80 to 120 man-hours (if based on secondary sources)
- Eight to twelve weeks, and 320 to 960 man-hours (if primary survey conducted)

Figure 33

Also, the competitors and characteristics of their equipment, identified in the second phase, are needed to structure the third phase.

The quantitative research hypotheses state which market segments will represent major, moderate, or minor potential for certain reasons. The reasons normally relate to: (a) combinations of physical, non-physical, economic, and technical requirements, and (b) the number of firms believed to have the characteristics.

As an example, firms having the greatest need for electro-optical gauging may be those using progressive dies to rapidly stamp and form small, expensive precision parts, such as gold-plated contacts for electrical connectors. The need is great because the parts move quickly from one stage of the die to the next, and misalignment or excessive wear in any stage can quickly result in production of costly scrap parts. On the other hand, there are other firms producing many components that must be assembled into different final parts. During manufacture, and just before assembly, it is necessary to quickly measure critical dimensions to ensure that automatic assembly operations will not be shut down by defective parts.

The main questions to be resolved are:

1. Is it possible, physically and technically, to make a general product that can handle the diverse requirements of such firms, or will several products be required?
2. Are there enough firms having the same needs to justify entering each segment of the market? It might be much more profitable to develop a less sophisticated system for a large product-market segment than to tackle the more complex requirements of a smaller segment.

Hypotheses should also be developed regarding where competition has already penetrated and why. The hypothesis may center on the belief that competition is strong in the segments with simple requirements because competing firms have historically been active in those markets and have excellent in-place service capabilities to serve those portions, but not others. Or the hypothesis may be that the technical sophistication demonstrated by competitive equipment may be grossly inadequate to meet requirements of other segments; thus, they have made very little penetration into those segments.

The number of individual segments that need investigation is determined by the number of hypotheses concerning important differences in need among the segments. Among industrial/commercial products, needs often are different among certain industries and sizes of firms within industries because of differences in product technology and manufacturing processes used. Combinations of these dimensions reflect differences in customer needs that provide the basis for product-market segmentation.

The time required to test quantitative hypotheses depends on whether adequate quantitative estimates can be made based on secondary sources, such as industry associations, commercial directories, government publications, and so forth. In most instances, the market potential estimates do not require exceptional precision on the upper limit. What is usually needed is assurance that the potential is at least some minimum size to justify the investment required and achieve sufficient economies of scale. If use of secondary sources is possible and sufficient, estimates usually take only a few weeks.

However, if primary data must be gathered through typical market research survey techniques, it is likely to require from four to twelve weeks, depending on the number of product-market segments to be covered. For industrial/commercial and consumer products, the actual survey work can usually be contracted out to a professional market research firm that maintains a database from which to draw samples and a trained staff of interviewers. The use of outside market research assistance can be both safe and efficient because the principal sources of error can be controlled and professionals used for data gathering.

Typically, the main sources of error in using outside market research are from not specifying precisely: (1) what information is needed, (2) from which individuals, within what departments, (3) in what size and type of firms, and (4) in which industries and geographic areas. These potential sources of error can be avoided with the Planned Innovation approach because all the information needed to design the quantitative survey is obtained (on purpose) in the range of requirements phase. The director of one market research firm who had just completed the quantitative phase of a Planned Innovation study commented that, "it was a joy" to do surveys with such complete guidance from the beginning.

The project can be conveniently and efficiently handed off from the sponsoring firm's opportunity analyst to an outside research firm when it is time for a questionnaire to be designed. Market research firms usually have considerable expertise in the design of such instruments once they know what information needs to be obtained from whom. The surveys usually require a short, structured questionnaire administered by personal interview or over the telephone to a sample appropriately stratified by product-market. We feel that mail surveys should almost never be used because the interviewer cannot ensure quality control on the data collected, and it is easy for copies of the questionnaire to end up in the hands of competitors.

Two questions arise at this point:

1. How can a small amount of information suffice at this important step?
2. Why is it not possible to obtain the same information earlier in the research process?

The answer to both questions is essentially the same. Because of the depth of understanding gained during the second phase, enough insight has been obtained to know which of many selected facts are key indicators of requirements. Therefore, it is only after gaining this depth of understanding that such a questionnaire could be designed.

The quantitative questionnaire is usually one to three pages in length and should be structured to facilitate obtaining the needed information in ten to fifteen minutes. Sometimes separate questionnaires (of approximately the same length) are needed for different product-market segments surveyed, if the terminology and requirements differ markedly among segments.

Design of a Stratified Random Sample

A sample is used when it is impractical to survey the entire population in the target product-market segments. For industrial/commercial markets, the number of firms or institutions in the population can number in the thousands. On the other hand, when developing products for military markets, the branches of the services (Navy, Air Force, etc.) and sub-units involved may range from less than six to as many as thirty. In many instances, when developing products for these markets, it is possible to survey every unit in the target market.

A random sample refers to the process by which the sample
drawn. The statistically random sampling process ensures that
every element in the population has a known probability of being
chosen (usually an equal probability within a stratum) and that the
selection of any one element does not affect the probability of se-
lecting any other. In short, the sample is an unbiased representation
of the population.

By way of contrast, recall that in selecting the sample in the
range of requirements phase, firms are selected that are believed to
have certain characteristics of special interest regarding the re-
quirements of the new product. Once a few firms with certain
characteristics have been selected and studied (such as small firms
with simple assembly operations), no more firms of that type need
be selected. We move on to purposely select a few firms with other
characteristics (such as large firms which have complex assembly
operations). When all the firms in the samples are gathered to-
gether, they represent what we want at that stage, the range of vari-
ation in requirements, but this total sample almost certainly does
not represent proportionately the characteristics of firms in the
total population. The sample has been biased (purposely) by the
selection process.

In the third phase of quantitative assessment, stratification is
used for greater efficiency in the sampling process. If every firm in
the population had basically the same characteristics of interest
(size, number of parts, method of production, etc.), it would not be
necessary to stratify the sample. A simple random sample consist-
ing of one respondent would suffice. On the other hand, where
there are a number of significant variations in the population that
affect the new product requirements, each of these variations must
be proportionately represented in the sample so that estimates of
the similar population proportions can be made with a suitable
level of statistical precision. To do this with one simple random
sample would require a huge sample size compared to a stratified
sample, which can give the same overall statistical precision.
Moreover, the critical statistical estimates usually involve the size
of certain individual product-market segments and the degree of
competitor penetration within the segments.

The selection of sample strata hinges on: (1) the significant variations among product-market segments, and (2) the expected degree of competition within each of them, all of which were or should have been identified in the second phase of research.

In designing the stratified sample for studying the requirements for automatic weighing and labeling machines for supermarkets and large grocery stores, equipment configurations were expected to vary according to meat volumes handled, and competitive penetration was expected to be greater in certain types of stores (independents, chains, cooperatives, etc.). Equipment configurations were also expected to be related to the size of the store. A three-by-three stratification according to these criteria was necessary, as shown in Figure 34.

As a result, the required sample size depended mainly on the degree of statistical precision needed in any one of the nine individual cells. In this case, it was decided that equal precision was desired in each cell. A sample size of approximately sixty was considered reasonable for each stratum, with a total sample of 9 x 60, or 540.

The level of precision required in each cell often varies considerably. It is likely that some cells are not as critical as others. In such a case, it would be more desirable to reallocate the sample (or reduce it) and tolerate the slightly larger estimating errors in the noncritical cells.

It does no good to select a basis for stratification that cannot be implemented. If the sample is being drawn from a master population roster, the database already must be categorized according to the basis for stratification chosen.

Three-By-Three Stratification

STORE TYPE

	Independent	Chain	Cooperative
Large	1	4	7
Medium	2	5	8
Small	3	6	9

Figure 34

What Should Be Accomplished in the Quantitative Confirmation Phase

The primary outputs from this third phase are the estimate of the market potential for each of the major segments and the measurement of the extent of competitive penetration in each segment. When these outputs are combined with the detailed requirements information from the range of requirements phase, intelligent decisions can be made concerning which segments offer the greatest relative profit potential, and what product configurations should be developed in order to compete effectively in each segment. Moreover, a meaningful return on investment calculation can be made to evaluate the investment decision.

If the market segments do not offer sufficient potential, or competition has already penetrated to such an extent that entry would be unprofitable, the project may be terminated or shelved. In most instances, the output of the quantitative confirmation phase provides the basis for planning the subsequent technical development program. The firm can proceed confidently with that program because the major cause of new product failure—the failure to analyze the market need in sufficient depth—has been eliminated.

Success is not virtually guaranteed at this point. There are a host of pitfalls to be avoided. There can still be technical problems, and there are other marketing strategy variables that must receive proper consideration. However, considerable information will have been obtained regarding the nature of promotion needed and appropriate channels of distribution to help in designing an appropriate marketing strategy and plan.

13

Application of Opportunity Analysis to Different Types of Products and Markets

The sequence of steps and the time required for opportunity analysis for both industrial/commercial and aerospace/defense product markets are practically identical, as shown in Figure 35. Note that the opportunity analyst must first define the opportunity, then compare it with the selection criteria, assist in assigning priority, and determine critical issues to guide the initial assessment phase. These two steps require about the same elapsed time and hours of effort.

Then, the opportunity analyst, or a team of analysts with the required technical background and expertise, must conduct a few selected interviews with knowledgeable, cooperative users who understand the unmet need and value. The time and effort required for industrial/commercial opportunities is about the same as that for aerospace/defense products. In both instances, the users having the greatest need, whether industrial or military, usually can be identified quickly. Critical hypotheses usually can be tested by conducting multiple interviews at the same (few) locations with informed persons with different functional expertise representing different levels of management, whether military or civilian.

The major differences between the analysis required in the two types of product-markets are reflected in the next two phases of the

Opportunity Analysis Sequence and Timing for Industrial/Commercial and Aerospace/Defense Products

Step	Elapsed Time (weeks)	Hours of Effort (hours)
1. Define opportunity	1	8–12
2. Compare with selection criteria and assign priority (compute rough ROI)	1	6–10
a. management review	1	5–10
3. Initial assessment phase	4–8	120–130
a. management review	1	10–20
SUBTOTAL:	(8–12)	(149–372)
4. Range of requirements phase	10–20	500–3000
a. management review	1	20–40
5. Quantitative confirmation phase		
• if based on secondary sources, or	2–4	40–120
• if based on primary research	8–12	320–960
• compute better ROI	2–3	40–120
a. management review	1	10–20
TOTAL (if all phases are needed)	(24–50)	(759–4512)
6. Establish R&D program		
7. Build prototype		
• engineering test		
8. Pilot production		
• test in market environment		
• verify market potential		
9. Finalize production model and marketing mix (compute best ROI)		
10. Start full-scale production and marketing		
• monitor actual vs. forecast sales		

Figure 35

opportunity analysis shown in the figure. The range of requirements phase takes about the same amount of elapsed time for both types of product-markets, but aerospace/defense products usually require more hours of effort near the upper end of the range shown.

Aerospace/defense product-markets are highly concentrated in terms of determining requirements and buying influences, but technologically, these products are often pushing the state-of-the-art, and they require more effort to define physical and technical requirements. Industrial/commercial markets are more diverse in terms of types of industry, sizes of firms, and geographies. They may require significant advances in technology, but, most often, they require only logical extensions or modifications of existing technologies and manufacturing processes. More effort is usually required to cover the breadth of industrial/commercial markets, but less to cover the technical and manufacturing requirements.

In recent years, there has been an emphasis on increasing the speed of new product developments. In many instances, it is possible to reduce the elapsed time needed in the range of requirements phase by increasing the levels of effort. For example, the elapsed time required by Lear Siegler for the range of requirements phase for the military aircraft Data Transfer System was only six weeks. Its derivative follow-up product, the Standard Flight Data Recorder, being a much greater technical challenge, required about fourteen weeks to determine the range of requirements. The development time from definition of idea to the pilot production model on the Data Transfer System was about eighteen months, compared to almost four years for the Standard Flight Data Recorder. The longer development time is typical for aerospace/defense products that begin by "pushing the envelope" of what is possible with available technology.

There can be considerable contrast in elapsed time and effort required for the quantitative confirmation stage for industrial/commercial versus aerospace/defense products. If adequate quantitative data can be obtained from secondary sources for industrial/commercial opportunities, the elapsed time (two to four weeks) and effort (40 to 120 hours of effort) are about the same as for aerospace/defense products, which almost always rely on secondary (usually government) sources. If adequate quantitative data are not available from secondary sources to estimate the potential for industrial/commercial product-markets, a primary data collection (survey research) effort will be required. The elapsed time for such surveys is typically eight to twelve weeks, requiring 320 to 960 hours of effort. Fortunately, this is the step which can be safely and economically subcontracted to a professional market research firm.

Quantification of aerospace/defense product-markets almost never requires a market survey. The reason is that the aerospace/defense product-markets are so concentrated that, after completing the range of requirements phase, the analyst will probably have talked to almost every key decision-maker. Although there may be uncertainty concerning the number of airplanes, tanks, missiles, or satellites to be built which incorporate the proposed system, the uncertainty cannot be reduced much further by additional research. The analyst should already have spoken to the people who have the best insights into further plans. Of course, additional investigation of international markets, such as NATO countries, may be appropriate. The latest published Department of Defense plans should always be checked, and input may be sought from the firm's political analyst in Washington for the latest projections on expenditures.

Traditional concepts of return on investment (ROI), such as payback period, discounted cash flow, net present value, and internal rate of return, can be applied with increasing degrees of precision along the new product development sequence. A rough estimate can be made after comparing the proposed opportunity with the selection criteria and assigning priority. A better estimate can be made at the conclusion of the quantitative confirmation research, and a best estimate can be made after the final production model of the product and marketing mix have been designed.

The accuracy of the estimates depends on the quality of information available for analysis. In all techniques for ROI analysis, the two items of information that most affect the accuracy of the ROI estimates—the sales forecast and the manufacturing costs—are also the most difficult to determine early in the new product development process.

At the end of the quantitative research, information is available concerning the total requirements for the product, as well as market size. Even though the technical development has not begun (with the possible exception of technical feasibility studies), a good base exists for estimating all remaining costs (R & D, production, and marketing), as well as the potential sales. Thus, the precision of the ROI estimate made at this point is much greater than is possible to achieve at the earlier steps.

Neither the time nor the manpower estimates shown in Figure 36 would apply to a major system development in either the industrial/commercial or aerospace/defense fields. We have seen as much as eighteen months and 20,000 to 30,000 hours of effort devoted to the requirements analysis for a major commercial computer system. A similar, or greater, effort would be expected for a major military system. The numbers shown in the figure are intended to be typical of a single product for a new or existing aircraft, tank, or other weapons system.

When the first five steps shown in Figure 35 have been completed, the development program can proceed confidently through the final five steps with very low probability of a major failure, because all critical issues have been resolved and all requirements identified. The logical sequence would be to establish (or finalize) R & D, then build prototypes, followed by pilot production and tests, then final production, development of marketing strategy, and, finally, full-scale production and marketing.

Parallel Activities Are Possible

In many instances, all activities need not follow such a logical sequence. As soon as the initial assessment has resolved all critical issues, preliminary technical research can begin, especially to confirm technical feasibility. As soon as the range of product-market requirements has been defined, technical research can be refined and production feasibility and costs studies can begin. When the quantitative confirmation has clarified the potential in each product-market and the degree of existing competitive inroads in each, the preliminary product-marketing strategy and planning activity can begin, and a reliable estimate of ROI can be made.

Determining Requirements for Consumer Products

The task of determining requirements for consumer products differs from industrial/commercial products in a significant number of ways. First, the emotive component of total value plays a much larger role, not only in the design of the product itself, but in important elements of the marketing mix, especially promotion, pricing, and channels of distribution (even in the choice of stores where the product can be purchased). Second, it is not as easy to tell which consumers will be in the target market for the proposed product, as it is with industrial/commercial products. Third, there are so many consumers to be considered, in comparison to the relatively few industrial/commercial customers. Fourth, there are usually close substitute products for any new ones developed, which places emphasis on evaluating the value of slight differences, which are often emotive in nature, rather than economic. These characteristics have led firms specializing in consumer products to develop a new product development sequence, such as that shown in Figure 36.

The significantly different characteristic of the consumer new product development sequence (in comparison to that shown in Figure 35 for industrial/commercial products) is the repeated, stimulus-

---

Typical New Product Development Sequence for Consumer Products

1. Define opportunity
   - Screen, Establish Priority

2. Concept test . . . .(SRMBI)

3. Start R D & E
   - Build prototype
   - Engineering test

4. Consumer test of prototype . . . .(SRMBI)
   - Estimate market potential
     (compute preliminary ROI)

5. Revise product
   - Retest with consumers . . . .(SRMBI)

6. Start pilot production of revised product
   - Engineering test of product model
   - Market test of key variations in marketing mix . . . .(SRMBI)
   - Verify market potential

7. Finalize product-marketing mix (compute final ROI)

8. Start full-scale production and marketing programs
   - Monitor actual vs. forecast sales . . . .(SRMBI)

SRMBI = Stimulus-response market-based input

Figure 36

response interaction with potential consumers at almost every stage in the process indicated by "SRMBI" (Stimulus-Response Market-Based Input) in Figure 36. This contrasts with an "AMBI" (Analytical Market-Based Input) approach for industrial/commercial and aerospace/defense products.

In the consumer product development process, after the opportunity (idea) has been selected for evaluation, the concept for the product is presented to potential customers for their evaluation and reaction. New product concepts can be presented in a variety of ways, ranging from a simple one-sentence description, to an artist drawing, or even a physical model of the proposed product. Upon receiving positive response to the concept, the technical development process is begun to develop and test a prototype of the product, so that a better representation of the product can be presented to consumers for their reaction, and suitable changes made based on those reactions. This sequence may be repeated several times before an acceptable product results and pilot production begins.

Preliminary estimates of market potential can be made after positive reaction is obtained to prototypes, and preliminary ROI calculations can be made as soon as final specifications have been decided upon. The primary purpose of step 6 is usually to produce enough of the product to conduct a market test of the product, together with its other marketing-mix variables, price, promotion, and place (channels), although further engineering tests may be made on products produced in the pilot run.

Again, repeated consumer reaction is solicited throughout the process, because there are emotive variables associated with each of these factors that determine the overall value of the product to the consumer. The marketing test is thus an evaluation of the entire marketing strategy, which is used as a final verification of market potential estimates. The remaining steps are to choose the final marketing mix (some changes may be indicated from the market test) and start the full-scale production and marketing programs.

A side-by-side comparison of the two typical sequences for new product development is shown in Figure 37. The figure shows the

Comparison of Industrial/Commercial, Aerospace/Defense vs. Consumer New Product Development Sequence

Industrial/Commercial, Aerospace/Defense

1. Define opportunity
2. Compare with selection criteria and assign priority; compute preliminary ROI
3. Initial assessment phase ....(AMBI)
4. Range of requirements phase ....(AMBI)
5. Quantitative confirmation phase ......(AMBI)
6. Establish R & D
7. Build prototypes
   - engineering tests
8. Pilot production of prototype
   - user test ....(SRMBI)
   - verify meets user need ....(AMBI)
9. Finalize production model and marketing mix
10. Start full-scale production and marketing programs
    - monitor actual vs. forecast sales (SRMBI)

Consumer

1. Define opportunity
   - screen, establish priority
2. Concept test ....(SRMBI)
3. Start R D & E
   - build prototype
   - engineering test
4. Consumer test of prototype ....(SRMBI)
   - estimate market potential (compute preliminary ROI)
5. Revise product
   - retest with consumers ......(SRMBI)
6. Start pilot production of revised product
   - engineering test of production model
   - market test of key variations in marketing mix................(SRMBI)
   - verify market potential
7. Finalize product-marketing mix (compute final ROI)
8. Start full-scale production and marketing programs
   - monitor actual vs. forecast sales (SRMBI)

AMBI = Analytical Market-Based Input
SRMBI = Stimulus-Response Market-Based Input

Figure 37

131

extensive use of analytical market-based input (AMBI) in the early and middle steps of the process for industrial/commercial and aerospace/defense products (steps 3, 4, 5, and 8). Stimulus-response market-based input (SRMBI) enters late in the sequence, at step 8, with the user test of prototypes and, finally, with user response to the full-scale production and marketing programs (step 10).

The larger components of emotive value in consumer products, and associated marketing mixes (especially advertising and promotion), require stimulus-response based market input throughout that sequence, as shown in the figure.

We are frequently asked, "Why not use this consumer sequence for industrial/commercial and even military products, as well?" The answer is simple: where the emotive component of value is not predominant in the product and marketing mix, the more direct approach is much quicker and less expensive. However, when a significant component of emotive value exists, that component of value should be evaluated with a stimulus-response interaction with appropriate personnel in the user organization.

Many mistakes are made in industrial and military product development activities by overlooking both the positive and negative aspects of emotive value, and many opportunities to provide valuable differentiating features are overlooked. Whenever an industrial/commercial or aerospace/defense product requires a human interface, such as a keyboard, or display of any kind, emotive factors are involved, and the proposed product features should be evaluated in a stimulus-response manner. For example, a firm manufacturing industrial circuit breakers for semi-tractor trailer rigs found that proper placement of attractively designed circuit breakers in the cab of a tractor could give it the appearance of the cockpit of a jet aircraft, a much more prestigious (and therefore valuable) environment for a truck driver.

The opportunity analysis procedures developed mainly for industrial/commercial and aerospace/defense products have been used to help with the development of many consumer products. The products have included a wide range of sporting goods, such as skis, tennis racquets, bicycles, golf clubs, sail boards, power boats, yachts, and motorcycles. Others include silicone sealants and caulking materials, plastic films and bags, to mention a few. In addition, the procedures have been used with the development of many products for end use by consumers, but purchased by an intermediate firm. These included automotive rear view mirrors and other automotive components, as well as gymnastics equipment and computer peripherals.

In every instance where opportunity analysis techniques were involved with firms developing consumer products, significant benefits were realized. First, the increased level of discipline in thought processes led to selecting and giving priority to opportunities that had a better chance of succeeding. Second, our format for definition of the idea or concepts brought immediate attention to the identification of the target market for the proposed product. Besides ensuring a market orientation, the definition process provided assurance that the persons selected for subsequent concept tests would indeed be members of the target market (and not the result of a "convenience sample," with little relevance to the intended target market). Third, the formulation of cause-effect hypothesis concerning unmet need and value proved to be of great value when focus groups were used to evaluate concepts.

Hypotheses concerning other critical issues, such as basis for competitive advantage, were handled via a few interviews with knowledgeable, cooperative people. The net result was that fewer iterations were needed in concept tests and better understanding was gained concerning reasons for total product-market requirements. The logic of our model provided a valuable check that all requirements had been met. This meant that the whole process could move ahead more confidently, including the formulation of marketing strategy for the market test and then full-scale introduction.

14

Implementing Planned Innovation to Achieve Multifunctional Involvement

The primary thrust of this book has been to explain what to do and why, rather than to present all of the details of how to implement the Planned Innovation system. Nevertheless, we feel that we should comment on what is required to implement the system, since many readers will have this question in mind.

We have been able to implement the system in almost every conceivable type of organization structure, industry, and size of firm. However, the degree of ease or difficulty in implementation depends largely on the existing corporate culture and the attitudes of management at all levels. But we have observed that it is possible to succeed with new product innovation in different organizational structures as long as certain criteria are met.

1. New product activity must be supported strongly by management from the top down.
2. Multifunctional involvement must be ensured.
3. Key analysts must have proper experience, education, and training.
4. A continuous flow of ideas must be nurtured and encouraged from personnel at all levels and in all functions.

Managerial Support Required

New product development activities have often been described as being disruptive of normal business operations. They cause changes to be made in every functional operation from engineering to manufacturing to marketing. Therefore, without strong support from management at all levels, new product innovation tends to wither on the vine.

It is especially necessary that top management define the overall thrust of the business by formulating statements of mission, financial goals, and functional objectives, and then communicate and interpret these statements to different (lower) levels of management. If several divisions or other business units exist, their management teams should prepare the same type of statements for their particular sub-units, together with opportunity selection criteria that explain the types of new product opportunities being sought.

Once missions, goals, objectives, and opportunity selection criteria have been established, they must be kept "fresh" by periodic review and updating at least annually, or whenever a major event occurs that requires a change in the course of the business.

In addition to communicating and interpreting the statements of direction and selection criteria, management must encourage and motivate others to tackle the changes ultimately required. Providing long-range financial support through appropriate allocation of resources to new product development activities is a major means of both support and encouragement. Another more subtle form of support needed from management is to understand the entire process and reinforce the discipline required by providing meaningful review and critique at key stages in the new product development process. Failure to do so tends to erode both the quality and motivation of new product activity.

Multifunctional Involvement

Early in the evolution of new product development procedures, there was a tendency to leave the entire job to research and engineering, and involve manufacturing, marketing, and finance at the end of the process. It was often said that the new product was "turned over" to manufacturing and marketing. This process resulted in the development of many products that did not have the proper levels of quality, or were difficult or expensive to manufacture, and/or did not meet unmet needs of sufficient value to users to provide a suitable profit. The net result was a high percentage of failures.

The more recent market-oriented focus of business has led to the involvement of all principal functions early in the process and throughout. There have been many benefits from this approach. It has resulted in a steady flow of ideas from all functions. It has shortened communication lines to the point that multifunction input to decisions is almost instantaneous. It has improved the decision-making process by helping to resolve critical issues early in the development process, thereby preventing mistakes, and it has permitted parallel development of engineering, manufacturing, and marketing plans early in the total process.

Multifunctional teams, assembled for each new product opportunity to be investigated, have proven to be an effective organizational means of accomplishing these objectives. But the objectives can be accomplished by having a separate department dedicated to new products, if that department and all functions appreciate the value of multifunctional input, and other means are provided to accomplish it, such as periodic review at each stage.

Qualification and Training of Analysts

Regardless of the method of organization used to achieve multifunctional involvement in the development process, not every member needs to be a professional analyst, but at least one member does. Someone needs to maintain the discipline of the process, to assure that the opportunity is carefully defined (with target market identified), then compared with the selection criteria and prioritized. Critical issues need to be identified and hypotheses framed to guide the initial assessment, determine the range of requirements, and develop quantitative confirmation of potential. Once technical development begins, someone needs to be watchful that all physical functional requirements will be met within the economic constraints identified. And someone needs to ensure that the total understanding of requirements to meet the need, including nonphysical functions, is reflected in the marketing strategy and plan.

In large, multidivisional firms with numerous concurrent new product developments, a large number of people should receive training as opportunity analysts as part of their career development. There should be at least one trained analyst on each product development team. Even small firms have found it desirable to have at least a few people specifically trained as opportunity analysts. The opportunity analyst need not be the head of a product development team, but must be an important member of the team. The opportunity analyst usually takes a leading role in the early stages of definition, prioritizing, and initial assessment of ideas. Thereafter, the analyst usually assumes a coordinating and supporting role, checking to see that everything is being done and that nothing major is being overlooked.

Because we were teaching the tools of opportunity analysis at the graduate level in business, we initially felt that such an analyst would ideally have a technical background plus an MBA. We have since found that this level and combination of education might better be described as desirable, but not essential. The essential requirement for an opportunity analyst is a logical, analytic frame of mind that, at the same time, does not squelch creative open-mindedness. We call it a "balanced brain," capable of using both the right and left sides.

We most often find good analysts to have a technical background, such as an engineer or chemist has. This is especially valuable in being able to communicate with those within and outside the firm regarding technical requirements. They may lack, however, the ability to interface effectively with marketing managers regarding the marketing mix requirements.

We have also found the same blend of analytic and creative thinking in college-educated persons with other degrees (for example, law degrees). A European analyst, originally trained as a lawyer, comments:

For me, the introduction to Planned Innovation as an opportunity analyst at a major American company's European headquarters constituted a lawyer's awakening to some of the harsh realities of business and markets. I had already worked in various parts of the chemicals industry as a legal advisor for more than 10 years, dealing with joint ventures, major contracts, acquisitions, intellectual property, and troublesome litigation. However, exposure to the business practices and the people involved in an industry does not necessarily bring an understanding of the ways in which that industry creates value. For the technical or professional specialist, with little knowledge of marketing and economic evaluation, Planned Innovation not only provides a detailed methodology for new product market analysis, but also indicates a fundamental "path to value" (as I would personally put it), which turns out to be a path applicable to many business and investment decision processes.

Because the opportunity analyst's job has so many facets, from technical analysis to conducting nondirective personal interviews and coordinating multifunctional activities, we compiled the ideal list of qualifications shown in Figure 38. We present it with the caveat that analysts should have as many of these qualifications as possible.

Because opportunity analysts become the "keepers of the discipline" in new product development, we encourage even the smallest firms to have at least two persons trained, so that they have another "professional" with whom to discuss important issues. Large firms may employ fifty to 100 analysts, depending on the amount of new product development. In such cases, we encourage the development of semicontinuous training programs, in-house and/or with the assistance of outside sources, to ensure a constant supply of analysts to replace those being promoted to other managerial positions. Analysts inevitably become increasingly valuable as they gain experience and, thus, become a prime source of managerial talent.

Maintaining the Flow of Ideas

We consider the maintenance of the flow of ideas for new products to be a prime management function. People are inherently creative. If a constant flow of good ideas is not forthcoming, look for what is blocking the flow.

Personnel Qualifications for
Opportunity Analysts

Education
   Bachelor's degree in engineering or other appropriate technical field, and some training in business such as MBA.

Experience
   A minimum of several years in an engineering or technical position, and several years in marketing or position requiring customer contact.

Stature
   Able to command respect and credibility from the CEO and all functional managers, both technical and nontechnical.

Intellectual Characteristics
   • Logical open-minded, realistic
   • Analytical, objective evaluator
   • Critical, questioning mind
   • Creative and innovative outlook

Emotional Characteristics
   • Ability to disdain the advocacy role for particular products
   • Self-motivated, conscious of time
   • Positive outlook; emotionally stable
   • Capable of finding new approach when things go wrong
   • Strength of purpose to keep digging to get correct answers
   • Ability to be satisfied with the right answer even if it is not the popular one

Interpersonal Skills
   • Excellent diplomatic skills
   • Tact, nonabrasiveness
   • Good communication skills (verbal and written) with technical and nontechnical persons
   • Ability to work in harmony with co-workers

Skills in Planning, Managing, and Directing
   • Good advance planner, ability to visualize all steps required in future activities
   • Ability to make efficient use of minimal resources
   • Ability to coordinate multiple activities
   • Appreciation of importance of attention to detail

Figure 38

There are usually two major reasons for such a blockage. First, we often find that top management has not done its job in defining the strategic thrust of the business and reducing it to an understandable set of opportunity selection criteria. The blockage is at the very source of ideas—all employees' brains—because they just don't know what to be looking for. It may be that management knows, but it has not been interpreted and communicated effectively to others within the organization in every function.

Often, the firm has been in the same business for many years and it may look like there are no new ideas possible. Recall that this was the case with the firm manufacturing gymnastics equipment. They had been making the same gymnastics equipment for years, and presumed that there was no opportunity for new products. Instead, new product suggestions centered on adding sports clothing and tennis shoes (products with which they had no experience or strength relative to competition in that field). It was only when management indicated they were looking for technological improvements in existing products that met (still) unmet needs that ideas emerged, and every product was improved, with increased profits.

Second, the blockage of ideas may be the result of a dam or series of dams in the stream somewhere. Symptoms of dams are frequent comments that "I have made several suggestions, but they don't listen to me, and I've stopped trying." Ideas must be stimulated, encouraged, and treated with respect when received. Every idea received which is not usable at that time deserves an explanation, and represents an opportunity for better explanation of what the firm is looking for. To do otherwise is to create another dam.

It is especially important to explain and interpret the selection criteria to those in contact with users, so that their selective perception can be tuned to identify customers' unmet needs of significant value. Persons in touch with users include sales and service personnel, installers, delivery personnel, and those providing technical support. Unmet needs can occur with the final user or with any of the elements of the distribution channel—retail stores, wholesale distribution, transportation and storage facilities, and so forth.

Members of the technical research and engineering staffs, including scientists, engineers, and technicians, comprise another principal source of ideas. These people are often cut off from firsthand knowledge of user problems and needs. Conscious effort is needed to include them occasionally in teams of analysts visiting users while researching new opportunities, so that their firsthand knowledge is refreshed.

Thus, maintaining the flow of ideas may not be seen as a management issue, but the flow depends greatly on how the process is organized, including the use of multifunctional teams, and on how ideas are treated when submitted. It is a managerial responsibility to ensure the flow by giving direction and stimulating response throughout the firm.

The aerospace executive who talked earlier about the "chicken test" adds this further comment on his experience with the process:

> Companies utilizing Planned Innovation successfully for new product/business development will undergo a transition from Opportunity Avoiders (finding excuses for not evaluating new opportunities) to Opportunity Absorbers (since they have a process which makes them confident in their decision-making—without fear of risk, they look for every opportunity that comes along). The result is that the "New Ventures Group," as we called it, always has more opportunities to evaluate than they have resources to do so.

Implementing the Planned Innovation System

Planned Innovation has a direct impact on corporate culture. The system will strengthen a culture characterized by open dialog, which seeks logical, rational understanding of business decisions. But the system will challenge and tend to upset a culture characterized by emotive reasoning, with decision-making based on positions of power, or political influence, without logical explanation. Planned Innovation has been characterized as a "mystique-destroyer" because it always seeks the truth, whatever it may be. Planned Innovation therefore has the attribute of always disclosing when the "Emperor has no clothes on."

Consequently, we do not recommend implementation of Planned Innovation in the emotive reasoning type of culture, unless the top two levels of management are dedicated to changing that corporate culture. Even when the management attitudes and culture are favorable, it always requires strong top management support to instill the added discipline needed in all functional areas. Therefore (and experience has confirmed this), the only way to successfully implement the system is from the top down.

Implementation should start with the top management team, and proceed to lower levels. In a large corporation with multiple groups and divisions, it is ideal to progress from the corporate to group to division level management. It is not necessary, however, to implement the system in all groups or divisions simultaneously to achieve beneficial results. It is very likely that the corporate culture and management attitudes will not be the same in all divisions, especially within large multinational corporations. Our modus operandi for years has been to expose all the management teams within a large corporation initially to the Planned Innovation system and let the individual teams (divisions) self-select whether they wanted to implement the process. We found that, if corporate top management was enthusiastically supportive, most business units ultimately came on board, even if it was years later.

Because of the intense logical discipline involved, Planned Innovation is not something conducive to force feeding. To do so is analogous to pushing a wet noodle uphill. Or, as we often found as university professors, it is no fun teaching required courses to students who don't want to learn.

Even when working with large multinational firms, we can usually feed the new techniques to management teams much faster than the tools can be absorbed and put to use. The corporate culture is thus changed, or reinforced, at a comfortable rate, usually over a period of years of such training, while moving from division to division and/or country to country. And, in every case, it is necessary to adjust the content, "dosage," and rate to the individual needs of separate business units.

When starting to implement Planned Innovation in a large corporation, each major business unit within the corporation needs to have a diagnostic exam, similar to a complete annual medical exam, to pinpoint what parts of the system are working and where things need to be fixed. Usually some aspects of the Planned Innovation system are already being implemented, needing only polishing and fine-tuning, while other elements are completely missing. We therefore recommend starting with a diagnostic review or audit of the activities needed for successful new product innovation, shown as a list of questions in Figure 39. This review needs to be made at the level of the overall corporation and at each major business unit (or division). Over the years, we have assisted many firms in conducting such audits and in devising seminars, workshops, and tutorial training programs to strengthen the many aspects of the innovation function.

The Planned Innovation Board

The Planned Innovation Board is a concept we have advanced as a means to continually monitor the innovative health of a corporation,

---

The Innovation Audit

1. Is disciplined reasoning process (re: new product innovation) understood and used at all managerial levels in all functions, re:
   a. appropriate models?
   b. scientific reasoning process?

2. Is a true market orientation reflected in planning and operations, re: existing and new businesses in all functions?

3. Were opportunity selection criteria developed by management with true consensus reflecting
   a. complete mission statements?
   b. strategic and tactical business objectives and financial goals?
   c. identification of strengths and weaknesses based on detailed examination of underlying capabilities?
   d. dynamic matching of resources to present and future opportunities?
   e. influence of major external trends?

4. Are new opportunity (product) developments guided by:
   a. proactive use of product selection criteria?
   b. determining total requirements?
   c. Are there a sufficient number of properly trained opportunity analysts?
   d. Does process provide discipline, structure, and unambiguous communication among functions?

5. Does the management and the organization support and encourage:
   a. the flow of new product ideas throughout the organization?
   b. multifunctional involvement in all stages of the development process?

Figure 39

and ensure that all aspects of Planned Innovation are implemented in a timely manner. Such boards are an outgrowth of technical boards we pioneered as a means to monitor the technological health of a corporation.[13]

Planned Innovation Boards, composed of three to five members, are assembled at the operating unit level. The members are knowledgeable about Planned Innovation philosophy, as well as the various functions of the operating unit. In instances where the needed creative members are not available in the overall corporation, it may be necessary to enlist the aid of known performers from the outside. Results with such boards formed and operated over the past two decades (at firms such as AMF, Genlyte, Reliance Electric, Whirlpool, and Briggs and Stratton) indicate a solid pattern of success. The greatest success has been realized where management has energetically implemented the results of the board.

Recurrent Training

It is well known in aviation circles that any pilot needs periodic recurrent training to stay sharp and proficient. This is especially true of those who fly sophisticated multiengine aircraft routinely in instrument-weather conditions. Specialists in recurrent training point out that even the best, most experienced pilots develop unsafe habits and shortcuts in an environment requiring strict adherence to disciplined procedures.

We have found the same need for recurrent training among practitioners of the Planned Innovation discipline. Even the best, most experienced men and women need tuning up periodically to stay sharp. This is effectively done through periodic review of opportunity selection criteria with top management teams and audits of reports from opportunity analysts. Classroom-like discussions based on actual case studies of completed new product projects provide a convenient vehicle to refresh training and correct any bad habits that have developed. Management participation in such sessions also provides an opportunity to demonstrate support for maintaining the beneficial discipline required.

For the management teams and analysts we have trained, it has usually been hard work, but extremely valuable to the firm and to the individuals personally. And to us, it has always been—and continues to be—an enjoyable and rewarding life's work, figuratively sitting in the right-hand seat of the cockpit, training and coaching executive pilots on numerous sure flights to successful new product innovation.

Epilogue

How Planned Innovation Provides Answers to Popular Myths Regarding New Product Innovation

Myths are intriguing because they all contain a grain of truth, which is the focal point of the myth. On the other hand, myths are not total truths because they leave out other important factors.

The Planned Innovation model of Requirements for Successful Innovation provides a convenient framework for examining myths concerning new product innovation. Recall that the fundamental model states that requirements for successful innovation can be represented as a solution space consisting of the overlap of the five basic domains of requirements, which results in nine areas of requirements. These nine areas offer a structural checklist that can provide the basis for reasoning or problem-solving regarding new product innovation:

Nine Areas of Requirements for Successful Innovation

1. Physical (product) functional need required in the market (such as computer hardware mainframe and accessories, etc.)
2. Nonphysical (product) functional need required in the target market (such as software, training, and service)
3. Economic value (source and amount) to the customer in the target market of meeting the physical and nonphysical functional needs

4. Emotive value (source and amount) to the customer in the target market of meeting the physical and nonphysical functional needs

5. Technical resources (type and amount of technology, personnel, and facilities) required for the technical research, development, and product design that will meet the physical and nonphysical functional product requirements within the constraints of the product's total economic and emotive value to the customer in the target market

6. Manufacturing resources (type and amount of resources required to manufacture the product given the required technology, levels of quality and volumes, while constrained by the economics of value in use to the customer in the target market)

7. Marketing and distribution (methods, type, and amount of resources required)

8. Basis for competitive opening (which might occur for any number of reasons, such as a new technical discovery making it possible to satisfy an unmet need, which cannot be met by any competitors, or the failure of a competitor's product to perform adequately)

9. Basis for competitive advantage (which may result from meeting the unmet need with a superior product providing greater value in use, protected by a group of patents in technical design or perhaps unique production technology and/or superiority in implementing one or more elements in the marketing strategy)

Using this framework for analysis, let us look at six myths. The first three are classic myths, all claiming to have the answer to success. The second three, of more recent origin, are also touted as containing the magical ingredient. The object of our analysis is to pinpoint what is the grain of truth and what is missing in each.

Myth 1: The Better Mousetrap

Almost everyone has heard of the first myth—the better mousetrap. This myth says that all you have to do to succeed in business is to build a better mousetrap and the world will beat a path to your door. Most examples cited in support of this myth represent major technical breakthroughs associated with a wide and intense demand for the product (for example, the electric light bulb, the telephone, the radio, and television).

This myth simply asserts that there is always an unmet need for a better product (requirements 1 and possibly 2 of the nine). Nothing is said about whether the better product has sufficient additional economic and emotive value for a large enough number of customers to justify the cost of technical development, manufacturing, and marketing (to let the world know you have a better product), and to provide means for obtaining it. Nothing is said about whether there is an opening for the new product (possibly because older products no longer work as mice are getting smarter, or because the world is becoming overrun with mice because of the failure of existing traps). No mention is made of how the competitive advantage from the better product will be sustained when competitors discover the new product is beginning to erode sales of their existing mousetrap products.

Yes, there is some truth in this myth. A key ingredient to successful new product innovation is the design of new products that meet unmet needs. But much more is required, as analysis with the model (checklist) shows.

Myth 2: Another Xerox

The second myth might be considered the first cousin of the better mousetrap myth. It states that the only worthwhile goal of the new product development function is to find the "super" product, a product so wonderful, its technology so powerful, its patent so strong, and its market so large that growth and profits are virtually automatic. The director of new products is told, "Find us another Xerox," because management believes that is the only path to truly great commercial success.

This myth is similar to the better mousetrap myth, in that the new product is so much "better" that it somehow guarantees that value will be realized by meeting both existing needs now fulfilled by present products, and meeting other unmet functional needs (requirements 1 through 4 of the nine) in markets of sufficient size to justify the cost of technical development, manufacturing technology and facilities, and appropriate marketing efforts to reach these (undefined) target markets (requirements 5 through 7).

Furthermore, the myth implies that the technical advancement underlying this new super product will be so great that it will help create competitive openings and provide a lasting competitive advantage from patents and other technical secrets. The bottom line on this analysis can be taken from the lyrics sung by Lancelot in the musical, *Camelot,* "But where in the world is there a man (firm) so extraordinaire?"

Occasionally there are major technical breakthroughs such as this. The invention of the electronic digital computer is another example like Xerox. But rarely do the original inventors have the match of resources to opportunity needed to exploit the power of these technical breakthroughs. The net result is that whole new industries are formed.

The real question to ask, though, is how likely is it that any firm, no matter how large, can make such advancements so frequently that corporate success is assured? In actuality, history shows that the probability of making regular, major breakthroughs is a slim one. Most breakthroughs are the result of a series of lesser events. Very often, the breakthrough, even though it was made possible by the efforts of many others, is credited to the person who refined or perfected the concept, and who appeared fairly late in its evolution. Recall that Guglielmo Marconi is generally considered the father of wireless telegraphy because he obtained the first patent in 1896. However, the body of technical knowledge that Marconi organized to produce the first practical system of wireless telegraphy was actually the result of many scientists who had been working for years on developments associated with radio transmission and reception.

We have observed a corollary pattern when dealing with product changes in mature markets. In such instances, a small increase in technical performance of the product may have great commercial significance. For example, the Hogan Golf Company was able to reduce total club weight by less than ten percent while maintaining the same swing weight with its "Legend" shafted clubs. The commercial result of this relatively small technological improvement enabled Hogan to more than triple its sales in three years, moving to number one in sales of golf clubs by pro shops.

The myth of another Xerox does great disservice to reality, since it diverts attention to the improbable instead of putting it where it belongs—on the commercially and technically probable.

Myth 3: The Gift of Genius

The third myth, the gift of genius, argues that successful new products result only from a special inner vision that allows one to grasp, in a twinkling, all the essential aspects of a new product. Edwin Herbert Land and his invention of the instant camera is a typical example cited by supporters of this myth. It emphasizes that all a firm has to do is to find the right person, turn him loose in the lab, and successful new products will begin to flow immediately.

Even if such a wonderfully qualified technician is found, the approach is usually doomed, because it ignores the central importance of developing products that meet market needs of sufficient value to enough potential customers (requirements 1 through 4 of the nine). We have found that such an approach generally leads to a proliferation of projects, resulting in spreading R & D resources too thin on too many projects for timely development and commercial success (requirements 5 through 7).

The myth also fosters the misconception that systematic procedures cannot be developed and applied to new product development activity. In one small firm manufacturing scientific instruments, we were able to refocus efforts on six out of eighteen slowly moving projects in the lab, resulting in dramatic acceleration in development and major growth in sales and profits. In a large, multidivisional firm, the central research lab was redirected to support projects with well-defined marketing requirements, with an overall increase in lab productivity of 200 percent, despite a reduction in staff.

Myth 4: The Lotto

This modern-day myth perpetuates the belief that success in new product innovation is inherently so unpredictable, difficult, time-consuming, or expensive that you might as well just roll the dice and hope to win the Lotto. As is the case with the Lotto, there have been winners, and they typically receive widespread publicity. Add to this the inherent excitement and thrill of gambling and winning, and you have a strong motivation on the part of some managers to take a chance and see if the product idea can succeed without having to go through the (relatively unexciting) mental effort, time, and expense of analysis and understanding.

Of course, the real issue is how much risk is appropriate for the firm to take, given the circumstances? Lacking the resources and/or capability to conduct the appropriate investigation, but having a good "gut feel" for the new product requirements, a manager may decide to take a gamble on a hunch.

Face facts: More gamblers are losers than winners. Having the tools and discipline to control the level of risk in new product innovation is just like having a diversified passing attack in football, with a variety of high-, medium-, and low-risk alternatives, each to be chosen depending on the circumstances.

Myth 5: All You Have to Do Is Ask Your Customer

As more firms are recognizing the importance of being market-oriented and designing products to meet market needs, it's easy to believe that all you have to do to understand market needs is to ask your customer (requirements 1 through 4). Asking the customers will always have eye-opening value in situations where the practice has been to *tell* the customers what is best for them, rather than *listen* to them identify their unmet needs and associated value.

The problem with this myth, as with almost all myths, is that it is partially true, but is not the whole truth. Taken at face value, asking customers is often very useful, especially when determining requirements for modifications and extensions of existing products. Customer experience with the existing product can provide a frame of reference for discussing possible modifications. Strongly felt unmet needs may have been elevated in the customers' minds to the level of "wants," which they can express.

However, even in these situations, results can be misleading, because different customers may view and use the same product differently and, therefore, have recognized wants that differ, with correspondingly wide differences in value (requirements 3 and 4). Furthermore, in military, industrial, and commercial markets, multiple buying influences, often at different managerial levels, must be considered when determining total product-market requirements. Knowing how and what to ask from whom is often a complex task, requiring depth of training and sophistication on the part of the analyst. Plus, the overriding question always remains: Will the existing customers be the customers for the modified product as well?

Asking customers about completely new products creates a host of different and even more complex tasks needed to extract meaningful information. Ideally, any firm would like to develop new products to meet unmet needs of high value to the potential customer where the understanding of the unmet need and value goes beyond the customer's own awareness. Products developed in this type of situation offer many advantages, especially lead time to develop, protect, and market the product without exposing the strategy to competition.

Research on the product requirements in these cases requires identifying the potential customers in the target market and then determining the existence of the unmet needs and the value to the customer, even when he or she does not (yet) recognize the need. Although this type of result may sound impossible to accomplish, it is not only possible, but done regularly by many we have taught. We first developed the techniques out of necessity to determine the requirements for military electronic countermeasures when the customer understood neither the technology, how it could be deployed, what it would do, nor what tactical or strategic value it would have. We have extended the application of the technique to many other military, industrial, commercial, and some consumer products in similar circumstances.

In each case, the research techniques were not ones of simply asking the customers. This is fruitless when the customers themselves understand neither the need nor its value when met.

Myth 6: The Alchemist Stone

Business executives logically seek to find methods to simplify the increasingly complex task of managing enterprises in a global environment of rapidly changing technology.

Perhaps the most insidious of present-day myths is the widespread belief that there is some simple management process which, if discovered, can lead to continual success in new product innovation. The alchemist stone myth does a great disservice by perpetuating the search for other myths, such as the previous five, all of which have some grain of truth, as discussed above, but not the whole truth. The alchemist stone myth leads management to search for a simplified process, rather than focus attention on understanding the inherently complex nature of the process and adapting appropriate procedures to address it as we have demonstrated in this book. It is analogous to believing that, in football, a simple passing attack with a few patterns is all that is needed for success against a sophisticated passing defense, capable of rapid change and adaptation to the offense.

We have found that it is possible to achieve continued success in new product innovation, but the techniques require in-depth understanding of requirements using a scientific, disciplined approach, which need not be expensive or exorbitantly time-consuming. Many have commented to us that the power of the Planned Innovation system lies in the straightforward elegant simplicity which it brings to such a complex business activity. Just as science was able to explain the weakness of the early alchemist approach to chemistry and provide a better paradigm for reasoning, so has the scientifically based Planned Innovation system provided a sure approach to predicting how to succeed with new product innovation with the necessary understanding missing from earlier alchemist-like managerial thinking.

As we have shown, myths may have appeal as a simple solution, but they contain only a grain of truth, insufficient to explain how to achieve success in new product innovation. A complex, multifunction undertaking in an environment of uncertainty and risks requires a system reflecting a sophistication and depth of understanding equal to the task.

Notes

1. "Marketers and Engineers Merge Talents: A New Approach to Product Research." *Transacta*, Michigan State University, Business Alumni Magazine, December 1970, p. 2.

2. *Planned Innovation, Second Edition, A Dynamic Approach to Strategic Planning and the Successful Development of New Products,* The University of Michigan Institute of Science and Technology, Industrial Development Division, 1981.

3. Figure 1. Sales of Donnelly Corporation. Donnelly Corporation, 1995 Annual Report. 414 East Fourth Street Holland, Michigan 49425-5368. USA.

4. E. Berry, *The Forward Pass in Football,* New York: A.S. Barnes & Co., 1921, p. 11.

5. E. Jerome McCarthy and William D. Perreault, Jr., *Basic Marketing: A Managerial Approach,* Homewood, IL: Richard D. Irwin, Inc., 1987.

6. Steven Toulmin, *Foresight and Understanding: An Enquiry into The Aims of Science,* New York: Harper Torchbooks, Harper & Row, 1963, p. 18 ff.

7. Toulmin, ibid, p. 28.

8. Israel M. Kirzner, *Discovery and the Capitalist Process,* Chicago, IL,: The University of Chicago Press, 1985, p. 68 ff.

9. McCarthy and Perreault, ibid.

10. McCarthy and Perreault, ibid.

11. C.K. Prahalad and Gary Hamel, "The Core Competence of the Corporation," *Harvard Business Review,* May–June 1990, p. 79 ff.

12. John R. Platt, "Strong Inference," *Science,* 16 October 1964, Volume 146, Number 3642, p. 347 ff.

13. Frank R. Bacon, Jr., and Thomas W. Butler, Jr., "The Technical Board," *Michigan Business Review,* XIII, No. 2 (March, 1971), 11–15.

Index

Accelerated sustained growth, 1, 3–5, 8
Adair, Red, 90
Alchemist stone myth, 154
All you have to do is ask your customer
    myth, 152–153
American Athletics, Inc., 5–6, 89
American Sports Products Group, Inc., 5
AMF, 84, 89, 101, 113, 144
Analysts, qualification and training of,
    136–139
Analytical market-based input (AMBI),
    130–132
Another Xerox myth, 149–151
Arithmetic techniques, 22–23

Bacon, Francis, 82
Bell and Howell, 62
Berry, Elmer, 10
Better mousetrap myth, 148–149
Blue jeans, hypothetical case of, 41–43,
    49–51
Bosnyak, Clive B., 7
Briggs and Stratton, 144
Business orientations:
   definition of, 39–40
   hypothetical example of, 41–43

Capabilities, defining, 67–73

Cause-effect, hypothesis of, 85–88, 133
Coca-Cola, 75
Competition, analysis of, 110, 112–113
Competitive advantage, 29, 30, 54, 55,
    74–75, 148–150
Competitive opening, 29, 30, 54, 55,
    73–74, 148
Competitive Requirements, 27–29
Cook, Rich, 3–5
Creative process, 57
Customer, definition of, 46–47, 49–51,
    69

Data Transfer Model, 62, 126
Donnelly Corporation, 3–5, 62, 70
Dow Chemical Company, 2–3, 7, 89

Economic Requirements, 27–29
Economic value, 28, 29, 31–34, 147, 149
Electronic computer industry, 75
Emotive value, 28–35, 128, 132, 148, 149
Enron Europe, Ltd., 89
Entrepreneurship, concept of, 31
External trends, selection criteria and,
    76–79

Fact, hypothesis of, 85–86
Faraday, Michael, 82

Financial goals statement, 64, 66
Functional need, definition of, 45–46
Functional objectives, role of, 64, 67
Functional product-market definition,
　44–45, 94, 95
Functional (Product) Requirements,
　27–29

Genlyte, 144
Geography, definition of, 47, 49–51, 69
Gift of genius myth, 151
Growth:
　accelerated sustained, 1, 3–5, 8
　through improvements in existing
　　products, 1, 5–6, 8

Hogan Golf Company, 150–151
Hypotheses, 23–24
　of cause-effect, 85–88, 133
　of fact, 85–86
　in initial assessment phase, 99–100,
　　106–107
　in quantitative confirmation of market
　　potential phase, 117–119
　in range of requirements phase,
　　107–108

Idea flow, maintaining, 138–141
Implementing Planned Innovation,
　134–145
　corporate culture and, 141–142
　maintaining idea flow, 138–141
　managerial support, 135
　multifunctional involvement, 135–136
　Planned Innovation Board, 143–144
　qualification and training of analysts,
　　136–139
　recurrent training, 144–145
Initial assessment phase of Opportunity
　Analysis, 91–103, 125
　decisive test of hypotheses, 99–100
　defining opportunity, 93–96
　formulating hypotheses based on criti-
　　cal issues, 98–99
　"going for the jugular," 100–102
　identifying critical issues, 98
　ultimate objective of, 102–103
　verifying selection criteria and estab-
　　lishing priority, 96–98

Innovation, distinguished from inven-
　tion, 10–11
Innovation Audit, 142–143

Kirzner, Israel, 31

Labor theory of value, 32
Land, Edwin Herbert, 151
Lear Siegler, Inc, 52, 62, 126
Levi Strauss, Inc., 41
Linear programming, 27
Lotto myth, 151–152

Mailmobile system, 62
Managerial support, 135
Manufacturing resources, 30, 148–150
Marconi, Guglielmo, 150
Marketing and distribution, 29, 30, 148,
　149
Marketing mix, 47–50, 130, 132
Marketing plan, 48–49, 51
Marketing strategy, 47–48, 51
Market orientation, 14–16, 39–52, 133
Market potential, quantitative confirma-
　tion of, 116–123
Market Requirements, 27–29
Market research techniques, 116,
　119–120
Matrix of information requirements,
　35–37
McCarthy, E. Jerome, 44
Mission statements, 64–66
　outline of, 65
Model Basis of Value, 21, 33, 94, 95
Model for Identifying Economic and
　Emotive Value, 31–35
Model of Requirements for Successful
　Innovation, 26–38, 94, 95, 147
Multifunctional involvement, 14, 18,
　135–136
Multiple hypotheses, method of, 82, 83
Myths:
　alchemist stone, 154
　all you have to do is ask your cus-
　　tomer, 152–153
　another Xerox, 149–151
　better mousetrap, 148–149
　gift of genius, 151
　Lotto, 151–152

Needs, identification of unmet, 12, 31–32
  hypothetical example of, 41–44
New product opportunity analysis (*see*
    Opportunity Analysis)
Nonphysical functional need, 28, 29,
    147

Opportunity Analysis, 132–133
  application of, 124–133
  benefit of hypotheses of cause-effect,
    85–88
  initial assessment phase, 91–103, 125
    decisive test of hypotheses, 99–100
    defining opportunity, 93–96
    formulating hypotheses based on
      critical issues, 98–99
    "going for the jugular," 100–102
    identifying critical issues, 98
    ultimate objective of, 102–103
    verifying selection criteria and es-
      tablishing priority, 96–98
  power of scientific thought process,
    80–90
  quantitative confirmation of market
    potential phase, 116–123, 125, 126,
    128
  range of requirements phase, 104–116,
    125, 127, 128
    analysis of, 105
    analysis of competition, 110,
      112–113
    questionnaire design, 109–111
    sample size required, 108–109
    testing hypotheses, 107–108
Opportunity selection criteria. *See* Selec-
    tion criteria

Pasteur, Louis, 82–83
Physical functional need, 28, 29, 147
Planned Innovation (*see also* Opportu-
    nity Analysis)
  analogy of commercial airline opera-
    tion and, 9–10
  answers to myths
    alchemist stone, 154
    all you have to do is ask your cus-
      tomer, 152–153
    another Xerox, 149–151
    better mousetrap, 148–149

    gift of genius, 151
    Lotto, 151–152
  Basis of Value Model, 21, 31–35
  defined, 9–12
  implementing, 134–145
    corporate culture and, 141–142
    maintaining idea flow, 138–141
    managerial support, 135
    multifunctional involvement,
      135–136
    Planned Innovation Board, 143–144
    qualification and training of ana-
      lysts, 136–139
    recurrent training, 144–145
  market orientation, 14–16, 39–52,
    133
  Model of Requirements for Successful
    Innovation, 26–38, 94, 95, 147
  multifunctional involvement, 14, 18,
    135–136
  scientific reasoning process, 13–15,
    17–25
  selection criteria, 14, 16–17, 36, 38,
    94, 95
    characterization of desirable oppor-
      tunity, 63
    competitive opening and advantage,
      73–75
    components of, 53–55
    defining capabilities, strengths, and
      weaknesses, 67–73
    external trends, 76–79
    financial goals statement, 64, 66
    integration of strategy and tactics,
      59–60
    issues involved in, 57–59
    matching resources to opportunities,
      54, 60–62
    mental energy and, 79
    mission statements, 64–66
    versus screening criteria, 55–57
    value of, 53–63
    verifying, 96–98
Planned Innovation Board, 143–144
Platt, John R., 82
Product, definition of, 45, 49–51, 69
Production orientation, 39–41, 45, 46,
    51
Product-market definition, 44–51

Quantitative confirmation of market potential phase of Opportunity Analysis, 116–123, 125, 126, 128
Questionnaire design in range of requirements phase, 109–111

Range of requirements phase of Opportunity Analysis, 104–116, 125, 127, 128
  analysis of, 105
  analysis of competition, 110, 112–113
  questionnaire design, 109–111
  sample size required, 108–109
  testing hypotheses, 107–108
R & D, providing guidance to, 2, 6–8
Recurrent training, 144–145
"Red Adair" assignments, 90
Reliance Electric, 144
Resource Requirements, 27–29
Resources, matching to opportunities, 54, 60–62
Return on investment (ROI), 127

Sales orientation, 40, 42, 45, 51
Sample size in range of requirements phase, 108–109
Science, general aim of, 21–22
Scientific process, concept of, 23–24
Scientific reasoning process, 13–15, 17–25, 80–90
Screening versus selection criteria, 55–57
Selection criteria, 14, 16–17, 36, 38, 94, 95
  characterization of desirable opportunity, 63
  competitive opening and advantage, 73–75
  components of, 53–55
  defining capabilities, strengths, and weaknesses, 67–73
  external trends, 76–79
  financial goals statement, 64, 66
  functional objectives, role of, 64, 67

integration of strategy and tactics, 59–60
issues involved in, 57–59
matching resources to opportunities, 54, 60–62
mental energy and, 79
mission statements, 64–66
versus screening criteria, 55–57
value of, 53–63
Selective perception, 55–56
Smith Industries, 52, 62
Solid-State Flight Data Recorders, 62, 126
Sorenson, Bill W., 5–6
Statistical (random) sampling techniques, 100, 121
Stevens, Greg, 2–3
Stimulus-response market-based input (SRMBI), 129–132
Strategy and tactics, integration of, 59–60
Stratified random sample, 120–122
Strauss, Levi, 41
Strengths, defining, 67–73
Strong inference, technique of, 82–85
Styles, Peter R., 89
Success rate, 1, 2–3, 7–8

Tactical failure and success, 61–62
Target market, 9, 12
Technical resources, 29, 30, 148–150
Toledo Scale, 74
Toulmin, Stephen, 21, 22

Value:
  economic, 28, 29, 31–34, 147, 149
  emotive, 28–35, 128, 132, 148, 149
  identification and capture of, 11–12, 31–35
  labor theory of, 32
  Model Basis of, 21, 33, 94, 95

Weaknesses, defining, 67–73
Whirlpool, 144